W9-CJY-651

Patterns of American Culture

Ethnography and Estrangement

University of Pennsylvania Press

Contemporary Ethnography Series

Paul Stoller and Dan Rose, General Editors

Patterns of American Culture

Ethnography & Estrangement

Dan Rose

upp

University of Pennsylvania Press
Philadelphia

The Masks copyright © 1984 by Dan Rose

Permission is acknowledged to quote material from the following sources.
Marcel Duchamp, *The Bride Stripped Bare by Her Bachelors, Even*, a typographic version by Richard Hamilton of Marcel Duchamp's Green Box, translated by George Heard Hamilton (New York: Jaap Rietman, 1976 [1960]). Reprinted by permission of Hansjorg Mayer, London, and Jaap Rietman, Inc., New York.

Wallace Stevens, *The Collected Poems: The First Collected Edition*, copyright © 1954 by Alfred A. Knopf. Reprinted by permission of Alfred A. Knopf, Inc.

Library of Congress Cataloging-in-Publication Data

Rose, Dan.
  Patterns of American culture: ethnography and estrangement

  (University of Pennsylvania Press contemporary
ethnography series)
  Includes bibliographical references and index.
    1. United States—Civilization.   2. United States—
Civilization—1945–   . 3. Ethnology—United States.
4. Corporations—United States.   5. Industry—Social
aspects—United States.   I. Title.   II. Series.
E169.1.R7752   1989   973   88-33964
ISBN 0-8122-8165-9
ISBN 0-8122-1285-1 (pbk.)

For
BEN MILLER

CONTENTS

Establish a society
in which the individual
has to pay for the air he breathes
(air meters; imprisonment
and rarified air, in
case of non-payment
simple asphyxiation if
necessary **(cut off the air)**

Marcel Duchamp

Thomas Smythe was the quintessential London merchant of the late sixteenth and early seventeenth centuries, and the mercantile icons that appear in this illustration—the anchored ship with furled sails, cask, bale, and bag of coins—suggest stability at the sites of exchange and trade and so typify his involvement in his age.

He exudes a confident affluence that is appropriate to his role as a cosmopolitan haberdasher in a city of growing international importance. The inscription that surrounds his coat of arms:

> The honourable Sr Thomas Smithe Knight, late Embassador from his Ma^stie to ye great Emperour of Russie, governor of ye Honble and famous Society of Marcha^nts tradinge to ye East Indies, Muscovy, the French and Somer Islands Company; Tresurer for Virginia, etc.

identifies him as the bridge person of Elizabeth's and James's reigns, the entrepreneur, the corporate executive at the juncture of the sixteenth and seventeenth centuries, but the person who also helped fund and administer the East India Company and the first successful Virginia colony: these were twin achievements—trade and settlement. Sir Thomas was the consummate organization man of his day, a merchant whose fortunes were made through import and export. Not only were his managerial skills eagerly sought, but in the case of the East India Company, Queen Elizabeth appointed him its first chief executive officer.

FACING PAGE 1. William Foster, *The John Company*. London: Bodley Head, 1926.

1
Colonization

The honourable Sr Thomas Smith Knight, late Embaf:ador from his Matie to ye great Emperour of Ruſſie,Gouernour of ye Honble and famous Societyes of Marchants tradinge to ye East-Indies,Muſcovy, the French and Somer Ilands Company: Treſurer for Virginia.etc.

Simon Paſſeus ſculp: Lond: Aᵒ.1616. Jo Woodall excudit

America is a country that was formed out of the private sector. It was composed at first of privately chartered corporations and proprietorships organized for an overriding purpose, to realize profits off the landscape of the New World. This impetus—this motive for acquiring material affluence—continues to drive us today. Adam Smith mentioned that, whereas the new settlements of the Greeks and Romans resulted from population growth, the reason for the formation of the British colonies was not so readily apparent. In retrospect the answer appears much clearer to us from our twentieth-century perspective: for many of the aggressive eighteenth-century English merchants and gentlemen entering a newly forming world market desired nothing more than to improve their fortunes and influence. From the collective efforts of the members of joint stock companies and the affluent proprietors of massive land tracts, the eastern seabord of British North America took shape as a highly managed outpost of the rapidly rising English entrepreneurial capitalists. Their worldly successes formed the very stuff of our contemporary institutions and has been preserved as implicit value in the most mundane experiences of our cultural life.

Patterns of American Culture simultaneously plays off the historical fact of colonization and treats the colony as the central metaphor. As I will show in Chapter 5, Wallace Stevens's poem *Comedian as the Letter C* provided a suggestion. Crispin, Stevens's comedian in the poem, founded a New World landscape of the poetic imagination; his discovery resonated first with the history of the thirteen colonies and then with modern American culture as Stevens witnessed it. I have borrowed liberally from Stevens and other poets in this narrative of contemporary discovery.

From the first successful colonization of Virginia as a privately chartered corporation, to the establishment of the last of the colonies, Pennsylvania, which was patented as a private proprietorship designed to market real estate, each of the British colonies was an initiative of the private sector. William Penn used propaganda techniques—advertising we would say now—to persuade a public.

> After consulting with shipmasters, merchants, American colonists, and weighty Friends, he published a ten-page tract, *Some Account of the Province of Pennsylvania in America*, which he then reworked and issued in abridged form as a broadside entitled *A Brief Account of the Province of Pennsylvania*.[1]

1. Richard S. Dunn, "Penny Wise and Pound Foolish: Penn as Businessman," in *The World of William Penn*, Richard S. Dunn and Mary Maples Dunn, eds. (Philadelphia: University of Pennsylvania Press, 1986), p.43.

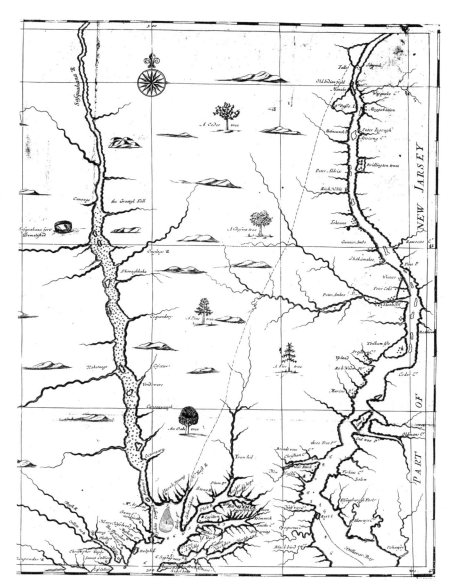

1. William Penn's Promotional Map. A Map of Some of the South and East Bounds of Pennsylvania in America, by John Thornton and John Seller, London, 1681. (Detail). Reprinted from Richard S. Dunn and Mary Maples Dunn, *The World of William Penn* (Philadelphia: University of Pennsylvania Press, 1986), p. 44.

By 1685 he had composed nine of these promotional pamphlets which had various guises and led various lives. One of the most important marketing devices was Penn's promotional map (Figure 1). In 1681 William Penn instructed four commissioners to survey land granted by King Charles II of England for a country town in the New World fifteen miles long fronting the Delaware River. The commissioners could not realize Penn's ambition for the siting of his city, because Dutch, English, and Swedish settlers had already laid claim to certain properties along the river. So the mechanism of private property foiled Penn's ideal plan, and the future city of Philadelphia was sited in a much narrower band of land between the Delaware and Schuylkill Rivers. The commissioners acquired only three percent of the frontage Penn wanted.

In a sense Penn's promotional map was a work of fiction, a piece of visual rhetoric intended to advance private enterprise. It showed a few property owners, not all of them. It conveyed a sense of openness, an invitation to settle in a vast, nearly uninhabited landscape. The boundaries of Penn's proprietorship were not yet adequately understood, and because of this map Penn operated on the mistaken assumption that he owned much of the property patented by Lord Baltimore.[2] The intent of the colonial proprietors whether as individuals or as members of joint-stock companies was to secure profits from the New World landholdings.

Two features of the private colonial corporations laid the foundations for our contemporary common weal: the charter of the company by the Crown which became a basis for the Constitution; and representative government, inaugurated as a management tool by the owners of the Virginia Company from their offices in London.

In the American Revolution it was as if the thirteen privately held ventures (though they were more than that by 1770) joined forces against Britain to shift their mode of existence from the private sector to their own self-authorized public sector, and from providing private goods to their customers to offering public goods to their new citizenry. It goes almost without saying that this deep split—often expressed as opposition between the private pursuit of profits and the public interest—reasserts itself again and again in the American consciousness.

* * *

To colonize British North America was to form a legally chartered company to monopolize well-defined real estate:

2. See Jean R. Soderlund, ed., *William Penn and the Founding of Pennsylvania: 1680–1684: A Documentary History* (Philadelphia: University of Pennsylvania Press, 1983), pp. 82ff.

From the time of Sir Humphrey Gilbert on, English monarchs regularly granted the organizers of colonizing expeditions a range of incentives including monopoly trading rights and large tracts of land in both North America and the West Indies. These rights and grants had great potential value and provided businessmen with a basis for attracting investors for joint-stock companies, which would open trade and establish settlements in the New World. The Virginia Company of London and the Massachusetts Bay Company were but two of the earliest such enterprises. Each was given territorial rights and an exclusive license to carry on trade; both became the founding agencies of the colonies that bear their names. They, in turn, recruited settlers by offering them the best possible inducement: land for farms. By the middle of the seventeenth century England claimed a string of colonies organized on the basis of mixed enterprise—part public, part private—on the coast of North America and in the Caribbean, from Boston to Barbados.[3]

* * *

A colony is formed to make profits from mining, planting and harvesting, manufacturing, and to trade on an international market[4] ———

A colony creates an internal market ———

To colonize—to continually create the new ———

Advertising incessantly creates new expectations and desires.

Theory colonizes new conceptual territory.[5] Scientists who develop new theories create possibilities for new combinations of matter, which can

3. John J. McCusker and Russell R. Menard, *The Economy of British America, 1607–1789* (Chapel Hill: University of North Carolina Press, 1985), p.45.
4. In his review of the Drake Manuscripts [Histoire Naturelle des Indes] from circa 1590—some of the earliest watercolors depicting the New World—Wilford wrote, "If these drawings are faithful to those impressions, late 16th-century Europeans were moved less by any esthetic joy in discovery or the romance of the exotic than by economic prospects. . . . for the most part, the European artists concentrated on such practical matters as Indians sowing grain, hunting with bow and arrow or collecting gold in streams." He continues, "The emphasis on animals, edible plants, slave activities and Spanish mining operations suggests that the manuscript . . . may have been intended as a kind of economic intelligence report." (John Noble Wilford, "Artists' First Brush with a Brave New World " *New York Times* [7 February 1988]). See also curator Verlyn Klinkenborg's, "The West Indies as Freshly Seen in the 16th Century," *Smithsonian Magazine* (January 1988):95.
5. See for example the convincing elaboration of this point in the Americanist William Goetzmann, *New Lands, New Men* (New York: Penguin, 1987). He introduces the

then be transformed into new technologies. Technology in turn provides the possibility for new commodities. New commodities are deployed to create new markets, new consumer preferences, new relations between persons, and new cultural possibilities.

It is as if the forces behind the formation of the new remain hidden to us, and that the sources of intellectual and technological production are obscured. The landscape of corporate research might as well be underground, it is so little available for review in everyday life.

* * *

America was composed of a collection of colonies. Today it bears an embedded desire and those social forms such as the corporation to create new resources and new markets within itself and outside itself as its most authentic mode of self-expression.

Frederic Maitland, the noted poltical theorist, observed, "for, when all is said, there seems to be a genus of which State and Corporation are species."[6]

* * *

We in America colonize and recolonize ourselves through endless efforts to introduce the new: new models of autos every year, new appliances, new names composed from computer-manipulated morphemes by which to identify new products, new clothing styles, new jobs, new houses—the list seems endless, even if the underlying forms of the activities are not. This making of the new is accomplished not by hardy entrepreneurial individuals, a mythologized Thomas Edison, for instance, but by corporations large and small. Indeed it is the corporate form that encases us in our everyday life in America. It is a form that extends back through the Virginia Company to Queen Elizabeth's chartered ships as extrusions of the Crown on the high seas and in alien ports, and to the Merchant Adventurers of England, who set up businesses and miniature polities in the foreign countries of the Continent during the sixteenth century.[7] Like our entrepreneurial predecessors,

---

book by outlining the culture of science: "In particular, we are able to see the history of the United States as it developed within the matrix of the culture of science and as one of the primary achievements of the Second Great Age of Discovery. America has indeed been 'exploration's nation'—a culture of endless possibilities that, in the spirit of both science and its component, exploration, continually looks forward in the direction of the new." (p.5)

6. Frederic Maitland, "Introduction," Otto Gierke, *Political Theories of the Middle Age* (Boston: Beacon Press, 1958), p.ix.

7. See Michael Nerlich, *Ideology of Adventure* (Minneapolis: University of Minnesota Press, 1987), pp.xxi, 52, 58, 108–82. Nerlich demonstrates that during the last millenium

we lead our lives within institutions that are convened through a legitimized body of rules and regulations, of corporate charters which are forerunners and parallels to the national constitution of the United States.

The interior relationship I find between our impetus to colonize and the corporate form as the way we characteristically organize ourselves to accomplish something is a result of the research presented in the following pages. Two excursions inform the text: The first is an ethnographic inquiry conducted over the last twenty years into American cultural life from a single point of view; the second is a picaresque allegory of ethnographic research (Chapter 6, The Masks).

I began ethnographic study as a graduate student within this country by living with black Americans in Philadelphia, Pennsylvania. They belonged to the working and welfare classes; to conduct my study, I labored and lived *on the street*. Every day I found myself engaged in a type of economic transaction that existed outside the familiar American middle class. Life in the streets was endless, mostly humorous, theater. My neighbors and I lived within but also marginal to American cultural and economic life. Two years of direct involvement gave me a look at America from a different vantage point: a view from the distressed margins of our society. Seeing things this way forced me to ask a further question: if many blacks, particularly the urban poor, organize their lives outside of the corporate mainstream, then how do other classes, more fully incorporated into society, organize their lives? What are the organizational features of the bustling affluent middle class and the more hidden upper strata of the very rich?

With the black families and individuals I witnessed the remnant lifeways brought about by an earlier colonial practice, slavery. The Africans were brought to the New World by private sector entrepreneurs. But with the end of slavery, blacks were never fully pulled into the enclosing private and public sectors of American life. It was from that mostly unincorporated location in black South Philadelphia that, through ethnographic inquiry, I moved inward and upward to a middle class anthracite coal mining city and then to a regional elite area west of Philadelphia. This motion from the economically unenfranchised toward some of the very richest American families was a voyage of professional discovery that forced me to confront, given my anthropological training, the organizational bases of American life.

---

the historical foundations of modernity were laid by the merging of chivalry and trade in the changing class system of the north European monarchies. The accomplishment became what we today experience as the endless refreshing of the new. One central—even determinative—mode of praxis that vitalized the present day has been *adventurism*. Colonization is one of the most exquisite manifestations of what Nerlich identified as commercially motivated adventure. The formation of the British colonies initiated a perpetual if displaced adventure in new, remote and quasi-bounded locations.

American and British anthropologists, since W. H. R. Rivers and his development of the geneological method, have searched the continents for the divere ways humans have organized themselves into societies. I brought those same methods and questions first to South Philadelphia, then to Hazleton, and then to Chadds Ford, Pennsylvania, as I inquisitively climbed around the American status system. My discovery of America is set off against the anthropological inquiry into world societies. As did my colleagues, I asked, How are the people of this place organized? For many, if not most, anthropologists, the primitive world was understood to be essentially formed on the basis of kinship. Day-to-day political and economic events and the greater or lesser rites of passages—of birth, initiation, marriage, and death—were found to be events ordered at the level of cultural codes. At the same time, however, these events invariably were played out through the social bonds of who was related to whom.

In America it does not get us very far to lay a grid of kinship over the society and postulate that the society is fundamentally ordered in that way. Little that we witness would correspond to kinship ties. The pressing question then becomes, What is the social order of contemporary America that corresponds to the social life of those smaller societies studied by anthropologists? The answer is at least in part, *corporations*, or more generally, the corporate form, the form whose motif in our culture is to always make the new, and in terms of the metaphor, to colonize.

The difference between what ethnographers have historically gone into the field to find, since Rivers, and what an ethnographer pursues in studying American culture, is that we in America cannot use kinship easily to explain very much about our way of life—though it has been tried. This difference, however, leads to a kind of alienation for the anthropologists who would devote their efforts to understanding the country—or Europe, for that matter. The estrangement is twofold. First, ideas that anthropologists have laboriously refined for the study of non-Western societies do not necessarily illuminate all that much here; and, second, life in a highly incorporated culture that endlessly destabilizes nature and material, history, symbols, places and persons, divorces us from the human continuities we vividly imagine to hold in earlier times and remoter places.

2
Estrangement and Spatial Inscription

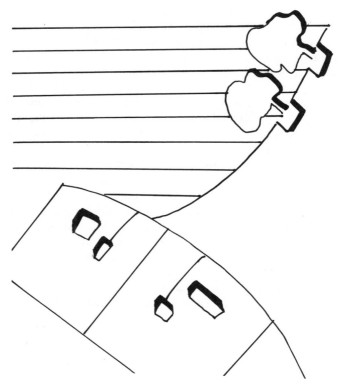

Landscape with no particular point of view. Sketch by the author.

The landscape is interior to the State.

We live in the suburbs. We are an anonymous American family living in the anonymous American suburbs. My wife, me, our two daughters.

Across the street a retired couple and their middle-aged son own a house. The retired father and the middle-aged son are both named Bill. Not Bill Senior and Bill Junior. They are both just Bill. At night, after the other lights are out in the house, the lamp in the window of young Bill's room shines from behind the boundary of trees that fronts their property and lines the road. Young Bill sells real estate on Philadelphia's Main Line and drives a freshly scrubbed black Chrysler station wagon with simulated wood on the sides. The house is two stories tall and painted white. It was built in the 1950s.

To our immediate left is a split level house, also painted white, trimmed in green, that was built in the 1960s. Between us is a decaying wooden fence and a cascade of forsythia that looks like a shower of brilliant yellow in the early spring. An old woman, Mrs. Smith, lives there alone. When she goes out shopping once a week she wears a black wig and carries a bag for groceries. I think she lives in silence in her split level, but when she meets my wife she begins to talk and tells long stories of her life years before. She lived with her mother in what is now our house. When she was a little girl, our house was a farmhouse. Her family pastured horses down the slope of our backyard. They owned a field across the street where the Bills now live. Her present house was built in the pear orchard, and now there is not a pear tree standing.

Next door to our right, smothered from view behind another fence and a tall stand of arborvitae, sits another house, really a stone barn made over into a house and painted white. A woman and her husband live there; they are middle-aged, their children in college. That house used to be the barn to the farm of which our house was the farmhouse. A small creek lies buried in pipe under our backyard and their backyard. We are at the top of a watershed; the small creek falls a hundred and fifty feet down a long hill and flows into Mill Creek at the bottom. There used to be numerous water-powered mills down there, and even whole villages, but now the ruins of old stone mill houses lurk nearly invisible behind ancient renegade domestic vegetation.

The houses are sited among the invisible ruins of former usual houses. Here there is a language game for the eyes

If I break my writing and go outdoors and plunge my hand into the dirt of the flower garden, I will feel soil that once belonged to the son of William Penn. The son owned this tract of land. History collapses and expands. He soon subdivided the property for farms and mills. The landscape was colonized and private as soon Penn bought it from the Indians. It is that kind of landscape now; our ownership inscribes the fence line, the hedgerow, the arborvitae and forsythia borders between properties, the visual markings and maskings of private property.

I am estranged in the American urban edge, in a small town that became a suburb north of Philadelphia. The process continues with new houses being completed every few weeks. As an anthropologist I live in a domestic exile, an estrangement, for unlike my peers I never left our America (the America of anthropologists) for Latin America, Africa, Asia, the Pacific, the remote highlands or lowlands, to study peoples without writing, or history or television.

My yard, enclosed by vegetation and fences, exemplifies one cut through America, a suburban one. As everywhere in America, there are laminations of history and culture on this plot of ground. Mrs. Smith, the aged woman living alone next door, told my wife about the well that stands open in an old stone well-house just off our back porch. In the era when our town was a small agricultural community, when people died the survivors would bring over the personal effects of the deceased and throw them down the well. Obviously the well was no longer used for human drinking water by that time, but it now provides an archaeology of local peoples' material remains, the little personal things, probably clothes, makeup, god knows what, at the bottom of the well. And there is the agricultural landscape, still visible as an underlying, almost secret stratum in the yard. There are tall black walnut trees, one with an American Wahoo splashed against it in some wooden inter-species embrace. The former owners, the family just before us, had added another layer of vegetation. He was a retired Swedish Lutheran minister and she was born in China, a child of Swedish Lutheran missionaries. They had tried to realize—though they would not have used these words—a landscape of personal memory and religious symbol. He had planted dogwoods and cedars of Lebanon, and they had bought potted Christmas trees which they planted in the yard. It was a landscape of religious and personal, of cultural, memory. More poignant, surely, was another planting. He had grown bamboo for her so that looking out the kitchen windows on three sides she could see miniature bamboo groves from each of the three aspects. By such an expression he had tried to help her unify past and present, remote cultural space with current domestic life. Against the driveway were a collection of water-smoothed stones she had nostalgically collected on her travels in America, but which were meant to evoke the smooth stones of a traditional Chinese garden.

Now my wife and I are secularizing our garden, dismantling the memories of the former owners—we've torn out the overgrown bamboo—and selecting our own plant materials. These kinds of changes are American activities, motion across a countryside that is like the restless movement of our people in general who reinscribe themselves in the habitations of others who were never known to them. This is the culture of motion with stability. For us and for our neighbors, the property lines remain but the vegetation mixes and the mnemonic undergoes transformation. Stability and change in the culture of market exchanges.

* * *

There are all too few inspired examples of what ethnographers can accomplish in this endlessly complicated culture, so, in a sense, there is an ongoing crisis for those cultural anthropologists who wish to devote their lives to the study of their own society. At the same time there remains a kind of obscurity, an obscurity partially insured by reading the literature on smaller and more distant cultures, as to how we ought to approach the understanding of ourselves. One of the reasons that American culture remains enigmatic to us is that it has inherited on a massive scale the corporation as a colonizing form, that ethnographic practice grew up in this colonizing milieu and is one of its intellectual products, and that our ethnographic inquiry is conducted from within institutions. Ethnographers are rewarded by persons like themselves who spend most of their working lives inside relatively large nonprofit corporations such as the university and the scholarly association, to mention two. The social forms that cage our intellectual activities remain all too invisible to us.

We must boldly identify the architectonic forms of our culture—Wittgenstein called them forms of life—and pursue the concealed energies within them even if in so doing we suffer the estrangement that results from intellectual and emotional dislocation and the palpable sense of discontinuity. At the same time that we quite rightly complain of estrangement as ethnographers (isn't it only another manifestation of what our suburban neighbors experience?) we gain a sense of the giddiness of the new, the sheer abundant cultural power unleashed in this New World, its dazzling array of consumables and its tapping into the most powerful of human creative performances in the new music, art, commercial sports and commercial messages, the movies, architecture, landscape design—who could complete the list?

A partial ethnography of America, then, as presented here, is the result of scholarly and poetic inquiry, an identification of the corporate form and its colonizing effects as central to our consciousness and as constraining to our research. One cannot wholly resist the explosive wallop with which we are hit by market culture despite the contradictory forces of abundant human creativity, disorienting discontinuities, and serious fractures. There is a self-conscious flipping in these pages between discovery, implicit critique, and the poetics of cultural inquiry, an inquiry that has alternately dipped resistantly into and skidded poetically on some of the aesthetic possibilities of the moment.

3
Pre-Capitalist
Exchanges

Three brothers on Easter Sunday, 1971. Photo by the author.

I was driving my Chevy through a late spring evening on the rain-slickened streets of South Philadelphia, down the narrow wetly shining streets boxed by three-story row houses. My wife, Karen, was sitting in the front seat next to me and the moving shadow from the windshield wiper stroked patterns on her face as we drove under the streetlights. We were listening to the news on the radio and waiting for the weather report, hoping that tomorrow would not be as miserable as this night. I told her that I would drop her off at the apartment and look for a place to park so that she wouldn't get drenched. We had just been out to dinner and as we entered the block where our apartment was located I started to watch for a parking spot. I passed one in front of the illegal numbers bank near the end of the block and only had to drive a little further on to our place.

We had lived in the neighborhood for a year and a half and had been studying the life of our neighbors who were black, and who were pretty much working class or on welfare, although there were many who were young and unemployed. Our neighbor across the street was a truckdriver; I worked for a middle-aged mechanic who had started his own business just the year before; other people we knew in the area were longshoremen, merchant seamen, and construction workers. One of the women who lived next door sorted vegetables in a food distribution warehouse.

I was trying not to skid on the slick steel rails of the trolley tracks as I pulled up to the apartment and braked the car to a stop. Karen, trying to dodge the raindrops, quickly ran to the door of the rowhouse that led to our second floor apartment. She unlocked it and disappeared up the stairs. After the door closed I turned around to look through a veil of rain washing down the rear window and backed the car slowly up the street near the numbers bank to the parking spot I had seen. I eased into it and never even noticed a black car which pulled quickly up behind me and stopped in such a way that I could not leave. As I started to get out of my Chevy, a cop, one of the elite Highway Patrol, commanded,

"Up against the car." There were two of them and I had no chance to do anything. They caught me completely by surprise, and I had been look-ing in the direction from which they had come; it was perfectly timed. I hoped they did not find something that I had, because if they did I would be spending the rest of the night, and probably far longer, in a Philadelphia jail; there was absolutely no bargaining, I knew, in this situation. As I'd seen in movies, I turned and put my hands on the roof of the car and spread my legs.

The one cop started to search me. He patted my chest under my jacket. I was wearing a Levi denim jacket that had a pocket over each breast, a short western style jacket that was meant to protect from the wind, but was no good for cold rain. I had it in the right breast pocket. As he patted my waist and down each leg to the ankles, the other cop, seeing I was giving no trouble, walked in a what seemed a deliberate swagger around to the back of the car.

Although they moved quickly they did not act rushed and I caught a good look, my first, at Police Commissioner Rizzo's dreaded Highway Patrol. I say "dreaded" because these were the elite cops, the ones who were lean and trim, who were noted for their sophisticated beatings of black men. They dressed in black leather, their boots—like storm troopers'—up to the knee.

The cop in back called out,

"Hey, these are Wisconsin plates."

I found my voice and figured that they had missed what I had desperately hoped they would not find and felt some remnant of confidence. It had all happened with phenomenal quickness and I had not been afraid at all. I am sure I did not have time to, had just gone with the flow of events until I could get my voice into it.

"What's going on?" I asked.

"Drugs," the guy next to me said.

The one who had looked at the license plates came up to stand next to me and asked,

"What are you doing here?"

"I live here. I just left my wife off and found this parking space. I'd like to get out of the rain."

"What about the plates," he insisted.

At that point I broke what had been until then my complete silence locally as to why I was living in South Philadelphia. Karen and I were doing ethnography as anthropologists—I was the anthropologist and she was helping by taking notes on her observations and involvements. None of our black neighbors had been told that I was conducting ethnography, we had not mentioned to anyone we lived near why we were there, I had gone to work for Telemachus Combs in his hole-in-the wall repair shop, then we had moved into the apartment next door. The first year we had just lived there and I had worked as a mechanic, and the second year Karen had begun to manage a sheet music business and I did some mechanical work and pickup jobs on the street. But to the cops I blurted out immediately,

"I'm a graduate student at the University of Pennsylvania and we live here while I'm finishing my graduate project." It was not quite true. I was living off a doctoral dissertation grant from the University of Pennsylvania while finishing dissertation research for my Ph.D. degree from the University of Wisconsin. Right then I was completely happy that I had not changed my license plates from Wisconsin to Pennsylvania. The cops bought my story and left satisfied with what I had told them.

They had not found the automatic pistol I carried with me all the time. It was a .25 caliber which that evening I had slid into the right breast pocket of my denim jacket, the safety off, six bullets in the clip, and one in the chamber. I had gotten it the year before because I had felt that I was in too many life-threatening situations with men my own age who carried pistols not to be armed like an equal. I had no license to carry the pistol and am certain that the Highway Patrolmen would have locked me up. In Philadelphia one can usually obtain a permit to carry a gun, if one routinely transports large amounts of money in the course of one's work. I had been told by people wise to the vagaries of acquiring permits that I would not be qualified for one. When I called my brother (who was under age and then had to ask my father) and asked him to buy me the gun, I was too impatient to wait for the permitting process. I reasoned that, if I were turned down, the local cops would watch out for me if I then carried an illegal weapon. At that same time a friend was studying Rizzo's cops. When I later told him that the Highway Patrolman failed to find my gun he told this to some of his friends on the Highway Patrol. He then reported to me that they were disbelieving that a couple of their best had missed a trick.

The more fateful possiblity, however, is that I would have been sentenced to a five year prison term. Carrying a weapon without a license is something that the cops and the courts take very seriously because too often guns are used against cops. I am uncertain that I would have been let off even with the reasons I could have claimed for myself. I was more than a little relieved that they missed the pistol in their search. Ethnography, as I was conducting it, was treacherous, and I had exaggerated the dangers to myself by carrying an illegal weapon.

Although I was not dealing drugs, I was intimately part of an underground economy, and of something far more interesting, something that I saw as a vestigial precapitalist system in black American urban life. The underground economy, a world without licenses or taxes to economic transactions, sheltered the kind of monetary and nonmonetary transactions that I am calling precapitalist. The black people whom I knew—mostly men— conducted a form of exchange that did not, does not now, closely resemble the capitalist mode of exchange of the north-European and American middle classes.

Through this story I want to introduce the reader to black South Philadelphia, from which vantage I began the tracings of autobiography that move outward to embrace white America. It is as if I stood inside a resistant, unincorporated black world and began to discover as an anthropologist a white world to which it was nevertheless fused. And then as I returned to white middle class life, I made the effort to discover the hidden order of

American life and concentrated unconsciously at first on its legally incorporated existence, and the effects of that existence on the spatial order of Philadelphia and its hinterland.

I worked in South Philadelphia in a black man's illegal or nonlegal shop, something both in and out of legally constituted America.

* * *

Karen and I lived with black people for two years, then moved to the countryside outside Philadelphia. A little more than a year later we moved back into the city to a white working class neighborhood and there our marriage broke up. I took the opportunity of being single once again to stay in the field as it were and studied a coal mining community, an agricultural area undergoing suburbanization which edged an upper class estate area. It was as if I were undertaking to move as a native observer in upward spiral of curiosity through cultural strata and trying to comprehend how we have evolved our national cultural space. These sites were within commuting distance from the University of Pennsylvania where I joined the faculty in 1974. Throughout the 1970s I engaged in continuous fieldwork. In retrospect, those studies can be seen as a kind of personal and professional quest for America visualized through anthropological eyes.

Our life with black people had exaggerated my concern with American culture, because I felt the exclusion and alienation that results from racism. It was evident everywhere that racist stonewalling had achieved its agenda of keeping many blacks from realizing their potential in American cultural life. In one of my field notes written when we were living in South Philadelphia between 1969 and 1971 I wrote that I needed to understand how the country was organized. I felt, as I lived and worked on the street, too remote from the organizational system of American society to comprehend first-hand how blacks were often excluded from the rest of the everyday life of the country.

Intellectually, I went through a dramatic shift from studying blacks to studying whites, and I simultaneously moved away from the disciplinary literatures on face-to-face interaction toward larger scale ideas and theories within anthropological thought.

* * *

Boycie was one of my friends in South Philadelphia. We had gotten to know each other by drinking together. He had taken me uninvited to a wake and later, on another occasion, I was present when he had publically argued with his landlord in front of a local crowd in what had amounted to a local lawsuit. On a hot August day, short of money, he and I had panhandled for quarters so we could go out drinking that evening. We were neatly stationed between the Martin Luther King, Jr., Plaza, a highrise slum clearance building, and a small corner grocery store. A steady stream of people left the Plaza to pick up some items of food or drink and we were in their way, not too far from the entrance to the convenience store.

Boycie had been a mechanic in the Korean War and after his discharge returned to Philadelphia, the city where he was born. His mother, and his mother's sister, and other relatives I knew about, lived scattered throughout black South Philadelphia. He was one of the few people I knew who had lived all their lives in the city. Our other neighbors seemed mostly to have migrated up from the Carolinas and Virginia. By the time I knew Boycie, he had fathered several children by a woman who lived in the Plaza. He told me that he turned over his entire disability check from the Army to her. When he needed money he *scrambled* for it. His right ankle was badly mangled—apparently from the war—and did not on the surface much resemble an ankle at all. For all that he neither limped nor complained about the pain. He was an excellent, intuitive mechanic, but he drank too much. He seemed to spend most of his time in the evenings in speakeasies. Speakeasies were unlicensed little enterprises usually run out of a woman's kitchen where one could buy a drink of beer or wine, and on rare occasions a platter of food.

I think Boycie lived several places at the same time. One evening he took me over to a weathered three-quarter ton Ford pickup truck. I asked him if it ran. He said it did but it needed *juice*, a battery. That night he wanted to show me the books he had stored in the truck, religious tracts of various kinds and a Bible. He said that he slept there, but I had trouble believing that he did it very often in winter because the cab of a pickup is very cold. I know that for a while he had a room in a boarding house. He lived for a time in a white businessman's storefront, and his clothes were stored—after he was evicted from his rooming house—at our place and at an old couple's house a block behind the Plaza. He might have slept there too, but he never slept at our apartment. The man for whom I worked in the auto repair shop, Telemachus, told me not to let Boycie keep his suits up in our apartment because he would try to move in. I let Boycie do it anyway, and he didn't try to move in. I know that Boycie's mother refused to let him keep much in her rooms. As far as I know the only thing of his she permitted there was a Polaroid picture of Karen and me that Boycie insisted he wanted to keep.

Boycie was probably an alcoholic, although I could not think of him in that way. When talking to Boycie and the other black people I was living with and studying, I felt as if I were lying on my back in the basement of our culture crushed by the weight of the stratified and affluent middle classes somewhere above me. I could not reach up to them, they were beyond my grasp.

A boy about eleven came by as we sat there, and Boycie asked him if he had any change. The boy by way of response said that he was on his way to the store, which implied he had no change, only bills. Boycie turned away from the boy and he and I continued to talk. A man in his early twenties stopped to talk. He carried a Bible and several other books. He asked Boycie if he wanted to buy a book that commented on the Scriptures. Boycie told the salesman that the books he had sold Boycie earlier were still in the pickup truck and he was reading through them slowly and had not finished. They talked for a few minutes and the man walked on. Boycie greeted others and asked for quarters. I sat next to him quietly when he talked to people he knew and was his conversationalist when there was no one nearby.

The same eleven year old boy returned from the store with groceries in his arms and Boycie asked him for any change he had. The boy said he had to take the change home to momma. Although he was not yet out of earshot Boycie turned to me and said, "That's my son. He's doing the right thing." Boycie was proud of the fact his son had not given him any change which showed that the boy minded his mother. He entered the project and disappeared from sight.

We collected enough quarters to get drunk that night on cheap, sweet wine.

Begging for quarters, I suppose, would be defined by the United States Internal Revenue Service as a part of the underground economy, but Boycie, who *scrambled* or hustled on a daily basis for what he needed to live, engaged in a local circular flow of money, goods, services, and communications that for the most part existed outside the purview of white society. In the literature on blacks, particularly in the autobiographies of pimps and players, this mode of exchange has been termed the *hustle*, and it connotes a con game in which the mark is taken. I want to expand thinking beyond the term the hustle and what it evokes. Because I lived on the street, entirely within the underground economy, except for my modest stipend from the university, I came to play with others according to the discourse of give and take. This form of interpersonal trade seemed to me to be language-like, a lingua franca among black people that could be found in western urban Africa, the Caribbean, and America's southern and northern black communities. When people needed and asked for something that another had, they received part of what they asked for. And when first parties wanted a return on what they had given, they only received partial repayment. This kernel of the exchange constituted the heart of the hustle and of everyday exchange relationships in which vital elements such as food and sex were given and received. This kernel interactive feature, which bound people up in larger and larger networks, was understandable by anyone engaging in them, but at the same time, everyone expressed dissatisfaction with what went on. No one was satisfied. Neither those who gave nor those who got. As a result people expressed hard feelings.

Along with the negative emotional tone to the constantly discounted trades, an instant credit system was instituted. It seems unlikely that people unhappy with what they had received would return for more, but that is exactly what did happen. Since both those who gave and those who received were continuously complaining to the community at large about how they had been short-changed, they constantly sought to obtain more from their exchange partners than they had received on the last round of give and take. I came to believe that lower class blacks, and certainly urban ones, could meet perfect strangers and in nearly any locale engage people there with the rudiments of the discourse of exchange I have just outlined. Indeed, the shop where I worked was run along the lines of the street hustle and I came to understand what went on from hard experience, even if I failed to develop a fluent ability in conducting the round of trades and expressions of hard feelings and demands for further consideration which the hustle exchanges required.

I would like to stress the instant credit quality of the hard feelings mode of the face-to-face economy. This is the way people became bonded over long periods of time. Because people felt they were owed by others, they were always, as it was said, *in one another's face*. Incredible intimacy was created by these exchanges, by the hard feelings and the endless discussions that attended them. Finally, there were no third parties who could, like some supreme judge, decide between competing claims. For this reason in part, I think, people were armed—and everyone was. Persons had to be their own collection agency for what was owed and had to be their own judge in the litigations that often enough attended the build up of hard feelings over unsatisfactory trades. No one seemed afraid to argue, and weapons were faced with an impunity that, as I witnessed with great sadness, ended all too often in death.

Here was an America that had not been completely infiltrated by middle class modes of exchange or the formal institutional frameworks, such as the courts, that evolved to control them. I was in an invisible zone of American life, as Ellison would understand; it was simply never glimpsed by whites in the middle classes. If working-class whites in contact with blacks knew about it and learned it, they did not write it up as contributions to ethnographic literature. I think part of the phenomenal resourcefulness of the black community in light of staggering relative scarcities in a capitalist consumer society is due to the instant credit quality of the face-to-face economy that involves everyone every day. Due to the barrier between races, a black cannot use the hard-feelings-mode of exchange with whites (or is the barrier there so blacks cannot?). You have to be in the community to feel the demand, pay what is requested, and ask for what you legitimately need at some later time.

* * *

Joyceann was sitting with Pig on the front step of her house just to the left of Karen's and my apartment step. I had worked that day for Telemachus and after a shower and a supper I felt much better. It was the thirtieth of July and hot, and I wanted to sit outside as the sun set to see what was happening and escape the heat in the upstairs rooms. Karen stayed upstairs with the television set on and was watching a program. The street was its own unscripted show. Women were walking together. Three men stood on the corner talking. There were two men standing in front of the bar with drinks in their hands and they moved their bodies to the music that poured out of the doorway. A large woman and a small man were sitting on the bench across the street where people waited for the trolley but they did not themselves get on when the trolley stopped. An old woman—everyone called her Momma—sat just visible behind her second story window across the street. Two of the longshoreman's sons nearly a block away were playing in front of their steps. A thirty-five-year old woman and her two young daughters, eleven and twelve years old, stood half way up the block and talked with a woman from a side street. Two men who roomed across the street sat on their boarding house steps in silence looking up and down periodically to see who they could see.

Joyceann turned to me from her conversation with Pig and asked if I wanted to play checkers. I said yes and went upstairs to get a checkerboard and checkers—the kind that were played on Fourteenth Street. As had others, I built my own checkerboard. [See Figure 2. In a rare break from mechanical work, Telemachus (far right) played checkers with Situation, a man of about seventy, who lived across the street. Moon, who was watching the action on the board, lived just above the repair shop with a black woman, Ivery Sims. She called Moon her ghost, partly because the two of them never appeared on the street at the same time and he only rarely came down from the upstairs apartment.] Black checker games were different than white ones. On the side and the bottom, two extra rows were added which made the board appreciably larger. Then an extra row of checkers was added for each player. This and several rule changes made for a very complex game. The most successful strategy seemed to be to form a wedge into

2. Telemachus and Situation Playing Checkers with Moon Looking On. Photograph by the author.

the opponent's pieces, capture them, get crowned, and clean up the board in a series of long, intricate sweeps.

Women tended not to play checkers, so I was always surprised when Joyceann suggested it. Joyceann was nineteen that year; her oldest child was a boy, Little James, who celebrated his second birthday that summer. Pig, who was talking to her in some kind of code (or dialect) I could not understand, was the brother of Bubu, the father of Little James. It was as if by Bubu's paternity that his brother Pig, his sisters Eve and Juanita, and his mother, Miz Mamie, could exercise rights of access to Joyceann's house. I say "exercise rights," because I never believed that Joyceann was all that close to Miz Mamie, a woman who was loud, profane, big-boned, and nearly white-skinned. Pig was that way too. He had a gap between his teeth, was very light-skinned and had a pugged nose. His nickname captured his physical looks. The whole family lived a block away in extreme conditions without running water or electricity.

I set up the checkerboard and we began to play next to her marble front step. I won the first game, drew the second, and she won three more games from me. Pig left as we started to play and returned with a portable radio tuned to WDAS, the main black radio station in Philadelphia, and with a quart of beer.

"You din' have any money a minute ago when I asked you to buy me some beer," she said to him.

"I picked up a *quiz*—" his voice trailed off.

"I had to ask Paul for the money for my beer," she told him. Paul was her mother's lover and stayed at their house most of the time. Joyceann and I did not exchange two words to one another as we played. By the end of the fifth game other people had gathered around and the game changed to cards, and I was eased to the side because I could not play as rapidly as the rest.

Karen and I always had difficulty talking with Joyceann and her mother or her extended family. We speculated with one another on the reason why. I bought some beer and sat and talked with other men who came up. Afterwards I went upstairs to the third floor and wrote fieldnotes. "We both feel that these people are extremely cool and believe themselves to be, if not higher status, then cooler than the others on the street. Either that or there is something else altogether which we haven't yet fathomed."

The next day I wrote cards which summarized some of the sense I had of the month of July. My central concern was with public space. "A bar, for example, will spill out onto the street as the drinkers form both an activity and an audience for any others on the street."

All summer long the street was perpetually alive. It was consummately an aesthetic space of dramatic activities, everyone was looking for whatever action there was with which to entertain themselves and above all to talk about until the topic wore away or was replaced by a more dramatic event.[1] All was performance, from the least nuance of Little James or someone walking down the street to a large argument that might include four or five households and fill the streets with an audience in a matter of minutes.

> A public argument between Telemachus and a customer which would have traffic backed up for a block
>
> Three girls jumping rope
>
> Boycie calling out his landlord for a public argument over access to his rooms
>
> People dancing in front of the auto repair shop to music from the radio
>
> Stogey Joe hitting a man with a pipe on the first floor over a hostile exchange of words
>
> Three men standing outside the bar near midnight and harmonizing
>
> Two old men fighting over a woman
>
> A man fatally shooting another in an argument over their children's fighting earlier in the day
>
> A mother stabbing her daughter because the daughter through neglect forced the mother to care for her infant
>
> Telemachus playing checkers in the mouth of the garage with Moon looking on

The metaphysic was one of continuous verbal and mimetic performance on the street, out in public, before others. Life was verbal and kinesic performance. To live was to set a play in motion—perhaps fateful, perhaps funny—and to follow where it led. Indeed, life was doubly aesthetic since song could mime and thereby critique street performance. This double aesthetic defined, in ways that go beyond this summary, the very heart of everyday life on the street.

These features, hustling which was itself public, and the performance of life as the way life had to be lived on Fourteenth Street, made for two dimensions unlike the bureaucratized and chronologically and behaviorally regimented everyday life of Anglo-America. Indeed white middle class conflicts with the black working and welfare class showed at these two points of contact, substantive face-to-face exchanges, and public verbal and musi-

---

1. For a fuller account, see Dan Rose, *Black American Street Life: South Philadelphia, 1969–1971* (Philadelphia: University of Pennsylvania Press, 1987), pp. 180ff.

cal performance. On Fourteenth Street hustling and black joking and play styles were met with complicated mutual embarrassments by both black and white. Whites couldn't sustain black joking routines and did not care for the music. Blacks were alienated from playing and joking with whites because it was difficult for white neighbors to develop the sophisticated cultural pieces of black public performance.

* * *

To many, Karen and I were hippies who had dropped out of white society to get ourselves together. As a result of our living the same lifestyle as our neighbors—me working next door to the apartment, sitting and playing games out front, Karen sitting on the front steps most of the summer, playing with the neighbor children—the distance between them and myself collapsed. I had no identity, no role to hide behind except that which I could pick up locally. At first, I worked twelve hour days in the repair shop and was exhausted by the sheer madness of trying to repair autos with poor tools, low-level skills, and the frustrated efforts of an ethnographic fieldworker.

The fact that I did not explicitly say that I was conducting anthropological fieldwork led to a rapid disintegration of my assumptions about what information I could gather. The worst worry was that I could not gather data, as we called it, that conformed to what anthropologists usually acquire. I could not use the tools in which I was trained: no interviews, no census, no key informants, no interrogating people about their assumptions, no eliciting dreams, no eliciting performances such as woofing, sounding, or playing the dozens. I feared that what was occurring was a complete lack of match between what I had read in graduate school and the entries in my fieldnotes. At the time I could think of no greater anxiety.

Over the years I began to feel that the logic of inquiry that I had learned from a graduate education of reading, seminars, and talking had been detonated by the field experience. Ethnography as knowledge about our own culture or about those of others opened up for me as a *radically fractured* way of life. Assumptions derived from reading ethnographies could not be played out in the field, given the covertness and lack of explicitness, and given my lack of the sacred status claimed by ethnographers for their inquisitive role. It took years to come to terms with such fundamental uncertainty. When I went to conduct fieldwork in the Pennsylvania coalfields (recorded in the next section), I tried to standardize and objectify my inquiry along the lines of traditional anthropological field research.

The received logic of inquiry, extremely simplified, can be evoked by a diagram. Each phrase represents an ethnographer's activity, and the arrow, a line, represents a logical progression.

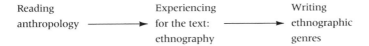

First, one becomes socialized in graduate school to one's profession, to the conduct of ethnography. The whole aim of this socialization is to duplicate at one level the achievements of the discipline, and at another level, to contribute in a unique way to the growth and development of knowledge. Second, one conducts inquiry along the lines one has read. Don Quixote, his servants firmly believed, had read too many books of knightly ventures. His obsessions with these escapades led Don Quixote to act them out in his own life. Graduate student socialization resembles the problem of reading Quixote's library. I simplify, of course, for it is as if to conduct ethnography requires that one construct a text from one's experiences with others, but from experiences carefully controlled by the profession. In a strong sense the way to process what one lives through in the field is normatively laid out in advance by peers, professors, monographs, articles, and books. In addition, one carefully grooms a persona, an identity which conforms to the expectations, but becomes the persona necessary to engage in certain experiences needed to craft the expected texts. Our documentations are forms of how we know. If inquiry does not conform to books one has read, the fear (perhaps the terrible reality), is that one's experiences will not be relevant for the texts one will write.

Third, success in crafting a text has everything to do with success in a career, since, with a few exceptions, careers are text-dependent. We write to be recognized and promoted, but we write also to confirm that identity we acquired in graduate school socialization. One assumes the culture of anthropologists in graduate school. Central to the culture and to the identity that goes with it are the field experiences for anthropological writing. Life chances within a career are closely associated with publishing books in genres that resemble, or at least address in a conforming way, the literature cited in the ones that preceded them. Important for my argument is that written words and careers take place within an academy that is crosscut by disciplines—and both the academy and disciplines are corporations, the context of ethnographic authority.

For me, ethnography as a way of life was radically broken open by the way I lived through the South Philadelphia fieldwork. As a result, I wonder about the form of life that ethnographers have cultivated since Malinowski. I join my voice with the growing number of those who question the assumptions and practices of anthropologists.[2] By such questioning I do not mean to engage in some self-indulgent reflexivity, but to query the construction of our largely taken-for-granted way of life so dependent on the written word and the cultural context of academic anthropology.

It seems that when young anthropologists leave graduate school for the field, thousands of possiblities await them: the people will be hostile, as the Nuer quite justifiably were to Evans-Pritchard, or the people one lives among may delight in telling stories for the anthropologist's publicly announced book. On the other hand, despite the ever-different empirical realities of field stays, there has been a dominant mode of authentication for anthropological work: the ethnographic monograph or book. The genre has been stable for quite some time, and its history, largely ignored, has existed longer than the academic discipline. To deal with the luxuriant diversity of human cultural life, anthropologists tended to standardize within a way of life, within the norms of the academy, with carefully conceived and highly monitored genres, the deeper identity of the writing and the experiences-for-the-writing. If the writing was not monolithic and was itself diverse, the diversity was carefully controlled, its boundaries visible to both readers and authors. The canon through this century has accumulated until we have between eight and ten thousand scientific anthropological books about other cultures (not counting dissertations, travel accounts, anthologies, etc.), recognizable as such in anthropology libraries, a corpus that has as much as anything else defined a discipline, a way of knowing, a way of experiencing—indeed, a way of life.

It is as if we know by our texts.

It is as if fieldwork is an extension of our anthropological, academic everyday life, a deformation of the outer skin of our culture of corporate life which never breaks. The skin does not rupture. In the field we are still academics, safe behind the membrane, we keep the same hours, do the same sorts of things, or do different things temporarily in order to advance our life chances back home. In brief, in the field we work. In the office we work. We work and we write.

With disguised field research, hiding in the workaday world of an auto repair shop, living on the street among consummate performers and travel-

2. On anthropologists' fieldwork involvements and creative confusions, see Clifford Geertz, "Waddling In," *Times Literary Supplement* (7 June 1985):623−24; on the assertion that the firm identity of the anthropologist centers on fieldwork, see James Boon, *Other Tribes, Other Scribes* (Cambridge: Cambridge University Press, 1982), p.8; and, echoing an earlier Geertz, that *writing* is what cultural anthropologists most characteristically do, see Jean-Paul Dumont, "Prologue to Ethnography or Prolegomena to Anthropography." *Ethos* 14, 4 (1986):352, 363.

ing through black urban space with Boycie, the whole structure of the research apparatus of traditional ethnography fell under scrutiny. I began to question our essential form of knowing, and more to the point began to wonder what effect our methods have on knowing cultural others and our own diversity in America. It became apparent that our forms of knowing were housed inside our institutional forms, forms of life that Telemachus and Boycie, and I when I was with them, enjoyed almost not at all.

One of the results of the estrangement I have experienced from the business-as-usual of ethnographic inquiry is to turn to the poets and artists. The quest is for juxtaposition and connection—trying to find common ground.[3] I will pick up the thematic element—that of a poetics of discovery of American cultural life—in the section on Chadds Ford.

* * *

Fifteen years later I am writing this in a suburb of Philadelphia where few black people live. Father Divine's estate is up the road and his heirs and their employees live there, but most of the black people I see in this area arrive by bus from Philadelphia and serve as domestics to the people who live nearby. The women who engage them pick them up at the bus stops in their Mercedes-Benzs and their Saabs. My adventures now seem distant from the well-rehearsed and well-executed ministrations of the Highway Patrol and the adventures with Boycie in the ominous shadow of Martin Luther King, Jr., Plaza.

One of the people I have gotten to know this year is Gaetano Ciccione, who lives a couple of blocks away. I think Gaetano has moved here to distance himself from his family, which, in the last generation moved from South Philadelphia to the suburbs near the Main Line. Three generations ago they were Sicilians. I cannot ask him if he is attempting to put space between himself and his relatives, but when I am with him I feel he has made that choice. One day he picked me up in his car and drove to show me the suburb where his uncles and cousins live and another suburb where his father lives. He has removed himself from that proximity by moving here. They all still work together, unhappily, in the same family firm, a very large kitchen utensil manufacturing plant in South Philadelphia. His maternal grandfather started the company and his father married into it. On his father's side there is a consanguineal closeness to a recently murdered Mafia family head from South Philadelphia, about which people speak only quietly, if at all, and about which he says nothing to me.

Last fall I was over at his house at dinnertime and he invited me to stay

---

3. Michael Jackson, *Barawa and the Ways Birds Fly in the Sky* (Washington, DC: Smithsonian Institution Press, 1986), p.4.

for pasta. I was happy to stay, and afterward we went into the basement, which had a garage at one end. Gleaming under the electric lights was a white 1961 250 Ferrari Testa Rosa. He opened the doors and hood and we looked into the interior and engine compartment. I asked if I could get in. He said, "Sure." My stereotype of the Ferrari was of an expensive, unreliable automobile, but my naive belief was soon shattered.

"Let's take the T. R. for a ride," he said. I could hear the enthusiasm for the idea in his voice. But he tempered the fun, or perhaps increased the pleasure, by explaining that he had imported it for a cousin who lived in Italy in order to sell it here, and it was not licensed or insured. He had a bank note on it and needed to sell it quickly in order to pay off the note. The bank had expressed a little reticence in advancing him the money as it was. But I said okay anyway, not having ridden in anything as exotic as this car. My only experience with high priced vehicles had been to ride briefly around Moline, Illinois, with the chairman of the board of John Deere and Company in his Rolls-Royce.

The Ferrari was nothing like the Rolls. As we drove into the night at a street corner not far from the house he said, "Watch this!" He put the car into first gear and slammed the accelerator to the floor. We accelerated like a rocket. I had never before felt anything like it in an automobile. By the time we arrived at the first turn off the road, less than a quarter mile, he had just shifted into second. He quickly braked, and downshifted, and then took the corner under power. "We were doing better than a hundred back there," he said. I found it plausible, but still incredible. It was indeed a world class machine and I began to understand the wild enthusiasm, the seductive power, the addictive quality, that captivates the Ferrari purists like some sweet opiate. He showed me that every Ferrari has a registered pedigree and is documented through the course of its existence, something like a yacht registry. An owner can look up a vehicle in Gerald Roush's, *Ferrari Market Letter*, a de facto American catalogue raisonné of Ferraris, and not only find out where it's been and who has owned it before but know as well that what fate holds in store for that car will one day be recorded in that book.

When hockey season rolled around, Gaetano asked me if I would like to go with him to a game. He said we would eat at Dante and Luigi's restaurant in South Philly and then go to the Spectrum to catch the Flyers. I liked the idea but did not anticipate before going that the seats at the game and the dinner were provided by the company. We left our suburb and he drove us down Philadelphia's treacherous Schuylkill Expressway. We turned off the expressway and cruised in his big Mercedes into South Philadelphia. It was as if I had been suddenly transported in time back to my fieldwork there fifteen years before. Then I had associated only with black people, I had not allowed myself to get to know any whites, including the Italian-Americans.

I had not gone exploring in white residential or commerical space. My research had the qualities of island ethnography, but my island had been inside black cultural life. Now I was cruising into South Philadelphia from the other side, from the white side. I was within a block of where I begged with Boycie, then as we drove to the factory where he showed me around before dinner, we were only two blocks away, but there was simultaneously a universe of cultural distance from the place where I had lived for two years and feared for the quality of my life from cops, coworkers, and adventurous neighbors. The epiphany was like some suddenly opened sky, some revelation that swept through me. Here I was in corporate America, in the white manufacturing, commercial, and residential space of the Italian-American community, and I realized with new intensity that there were two worlds: the private, chartered corporate life of those who manufactured and ran businesses, and the life of those who in remarkable and distressing contrast hustled on the street for the necessities, people who, like Boycie, *were essentially and in nearly every way outside corporate America.* This polarity cut through the black working and welfare class. Gaetano's family owned their own business, and it seemed that nearly all the families of the nearby Italian Market had a legally incorporated concern, whether or not it was large or small scale, or trafficked in legal or illegal goods. And there seemed at that moment in moving from white to black driving into South Philadelphia as a white person and not as a black person (which in a sense was the way I had absurdly moved fifteen years before) I was confronted with a fine but ungiving dividing line between the street hustles and face-to-face exchange economy of Boycie and most of the others I knew, the theatrical life of performance on the street, and the white shop and corporation owners that began a mere block away.

4
Capitalist Social Forms

A Ford bus had been converted into a general store—private enterprise on wheels. The driver made the rounds of the hard-to-reach patch towns of the coal fields. A patch town was sited next to a strip mine or at the entrance to a deep mine. The properties and the houses of the patch towns before World War II were entirely owned by mining corporations. Photo by the author.

In the middle of winter in Philadelphia in 1973–74, I got into my Jeep and warmed it up, put it into four wheel drive and maneuvered the wet streets to Germantown where I picked up Jon Berger. We drove north of the city up the Northeast Extension of the Pennsylvania Turnpike toward Hazleton, an anthracite coal mining city in the Appalachian mountains which on a good day was more than two hours away by car. As we drove, a light rain turned to sleet and then a fine snow as we climbed into the mountains. I had to get out a couple of times and scrape ice from the windshield in order to see where I was going, and it was useful to have the Jeep. Jon had made an appointment for us to talk with Nick Marsilio, a builder whose family firm was in Hazleton. Marsilio was an active and powerful member in Democratic Party politics and the Hazleton Chamber of Commerce.

I had suggested to Jon that we conduct ethnographic fieldwork in the southern end of Luzerne County, Pennsylvania, where Hazleton was located. By understanding the place we could use it in our teaching. We had both just joined the faculty of Landscape Architecture and Regional Planning at the University of Pennsylvania. Jon was a gifted natural observer, had been a member of the Peace Corps, and was trained in environmental planning. But he had not previously undertaken systematic ethnographic inquiry. My purpose in the research project in southern Luzerne County was a continuation of my desire to make anthropology as a scholarly pursuit more central to the study of our own culture. I had an equally strong urge to retrain my approach to ethnography by changing from face-to-face studies to something larger. By joining the landscape department, I hoped to move environmental anthropology as close to ecological planning and design as I could. I wanted to fuse the two, if possible, within an educational framework. At that time, 1974, due to Ian McHarg's efforts, the landscape department was the foremost environmental planning and design program in the country, perhaps the world. Within the department there was a vision and a demand to add an anthropological study of humans to the understanding of the natural environment afforded by natural sciences, which was the historical strength of the department.

When Jon Berger and I met during the break between the fall and spring terms in my apartment in Philadelphia, I outlined for him a proposed study of the political economy of southern Luzerne County. I had read the literature on ecological anthropology and used Rappaport's *Pigs for the Ancestors*[1] and the various articles by Julian Steward on cultural ecology. The trouble with the anthropological literature at that time was that it dealt with behavioral patterns but not with institutional structures. Everywhere I

1. Roy Rappaport, *Pigs for the Ancestors* (New Haven, Conn.: Yale University Press, 1968).

looked in America I found institutions. If we had tried to concentrate exclusively on behavioral patterns we would haved drowned in readily observable activities with no sense of priorities as to which behavioral patterns of the infinite variety we should examine. What Steward called the culture core—that set of exploitive practices and techniques at the interface of nature and culture—I had to translate into the scale of America social life.[2]

Marx's writings, rather than those of Rappaport and Steward, led me closer to the scale for a framework on which to hang naturalistic description. In *A Contribution to the Critique of Political Economy*,[3] Marx examined production, distribution, exchange, and consumption. I discussed with Berger the possibility that we could look at the human occupation of Hazleton and southern Luzerne County as a great edifice of human invention, a political economy machine for giving and taking energy from the environment, and creating as it did so the particular patterns on the landscape, the forms of settlements, and use of the soils, hydrology, vegetation, and geology. Berger brought a knowledge of the natural systems to our discussions and our later reconnaissance and extensive interviews, while I was intent on finding the social forms that used and thereby shaped the arrangement of naturally occurring flora and fauna.

To Marx's production, distribution, exchange, and consumption I needed to add technology, for it was through science applied to ever more efficient technology that human institutions exploited the natural environment. At the same time I had to add the natural environment to Marx's production processes, because production is production of something and that something tended to be grown or mined or at least placed upon the ground. Berger added the knowledge of a litany of natural factors that we could systematically examine in relation to those institutions, such as the coal companies, which used geology, for example, for economic purposes. Geology became coal, climate became fog, the fog, indeed, figured prominently in the lobbying over the siting of the interstate highway system in the region.

There was one other notable addition to Marx's descriptive political economy that was needed, and it was a sense of those structures, not necessarily coterminous with a vaguely identified class of people, which guided the whole human machine in its economic exploitation of the natural environment. The guidance structures I considered were also institutions and made up of three sectors, the private and for-profit sector, the public and governmental sector, and the not-for-profit or nonprofit sector. These guid-

2. Dan Rose, *Energy Transition and the Local Community* (Philadelphia: University of Pennsylvania Press, 1981).

3. Karl Marx, *A Contribution to the Critique of Political Economy* (New York: International Publishers, 1970).

ing features of the social system I later came to call controlling mechanisms, for indeed they seemed to act to command, albeit imperfectly, flows of energy, matter, people, machinery, products, money, and information.

At the kitchen table in my apartment earlier, Jon and I had agreed to interview for knowledge of the political economy, and especially for how people used their natural environments. We internalized a hidden agenda and then interviewed, usually without pencil and paper present, people we found who could help us.

Although I had been alienated from ethnographic method through the research in South Philadelphia, in Hazleton I attempted to reconfigure thought and practice by using theory consciously prior to the engagement in fieldwork so that the entire effort would be theory-driven. The choice to follow an explicitly standardized research agenda was an act of compensation for the earlier disorientation and imprisoning smallness of scale brought about in part by concealed research.

When we arrived in Hazleton on that wintry day the Jeep was coated with ice and our host, Nick, was surprised to see us.

"I didn't think you'd make it through all this snow," he remarked; but how could he know that Berger and I were unrelenting fieldworkers? Nick suggested that we go to Gus Genetti's Tyrolean Restaurant for lunch, which we did, and we talked for two hours in the nearly deserted dining room. The snowfall steadily built up, the weather really was inhospitable, and business remained at a standstill. As we talked we asked Nick a number of questions, and one of the answers he gave set up the subsequent research I did with Berger and later alone.

"After the war," he explained, "we saw our kids moving away, and with the mines closing, we didn't have any customers for our businesses. It was either move away ourselves and set up business someplace else, or find some way of keeping our children and the unemployed coalminers here."

It was the way the bourgeoisie found customers that struck me as a powerful statement, the creation of demand, a kind of colonization, and it was the locally formulated response, Nick's representative point of view to the challenge of resource decline in coal and outmigration, that helped immeasurably to set the empirical agenda for the ethnographic study.

At the end of our conversation he asked, "When are you fellows going to start interviewing me?" I replied, "We just did, thanks," and Berger and I smiled at each other.

WHAT I FOUND

After World War II, Hazleton and the surrounding townships, like much of the rest of the country, discovered itself in a historical moment without precedent in its past. During the rise of anthracite coal mining through most of the nineteenth century and its peak of production in the mid 1920s, small and large scale extraction industries had dominated the mountains. Their employees consumed the agricultural produce of the valleys. By the turn of the twentieth century, large corporations controlled by New York banks and New York and Philadelphia railroad interests commanded the economy of the coalfields of eastern Pennsylvania through ownership of extensive land holdings and mines. Coal, it was widely observed, was king.

With the stock market crash of 1929, anthracite production fell into a steep decline from which it never recovered. After World War II the anthracite industry collapsed into little more than a disorganized complex of cottage industries, the large mining corporations were shoved aside by petroleum and the railroad corporations by automobiles. They disintegrated through bankruptcies and restructuring. A major shift had occurred in the American economy from the energy base in coal toward an energy base in petroleum. The transportation, domestic and commercial heating, and electrical generation sectors of the economy were completely transformed with the attendant massive disruptions in settlement patterns and communications. The truck and automobile, most notably, replaced the train and horse.

The businessmen of Hazleton, after returning from the European and Asian theaters, found for the first time, and to their amazement, that it was they, by and large, who owned the larger firms in the coalfields, in the turbulent wake of the once ruling extraction corporations which in their own demise had withdrawn from anthracite. The viable coal mining operations in the country were found in the bituminous fields of Appalachia, including Western Pennsylvania. As a result, population decline and unemployment plagued the region. Those who sold goods and services found that they would soon run out of economically viable customers.

For nearly a decade the business people struggled with the new realities until 1956 when a not-for-profit corporation was established by the leaders of the business community—department store owners and other merchants, doctors, a clergyman or two, but not bankers or mine owners—as a spin-off from the Chamber of Commerce. Chambers of Commerce in America have, far beyond the boosterism image easily dismissed by the intellectuals, devoted themselves to the economic vitality of their collective concerns, their communities, and their hinterlands. As Nick pointed out to us, the new community corporation, named CAN DO by its members, had as its explicit goal the creating of jobs for local men in order to reestablish a viable economy for the vending of members' goods and services. They inaugurated an industrial park strategy: they bought land and developed infrastructure to attract firms of industries in a phase of postwar expansion.

CAN DO was a corporation among corporations, a kind of ad hoc trade association, an interest group. It was less overtly ideological and more overtly pragmatic than a political party; its scope was relatively narrow, its self-announced goal was to attract male-employing industries.

Internally CAN DO looked like other American corporations: the owners, or stakeholders, were the bond holders and cash contributors from the community and it included both individuals and other corporations in the community—the not-for-profit ones such as the Kiwanis and Lions' Club—the board of directors was comprised of the organizers of CAN DO but included places for those who had made outstanding financial contributions. Various associations and companies could buy themselves a directorship and influence the course of policy formation within CAN DO; there was an executive committee, the internal core of the merchants and professionals taken largely from the Chamber of Commerce membership who ran the day-to-day affairs, courted corporations to locate in Hazleton, worked through local radio and newspapers to galvanize public opinion within Hazleton to support CAN DO aims, and lobbied at local, state, and federal levels to secure subsidized industrial loans, and to site infrastructure locally such as the interstate highway. Within CAN DO—and there has been a long history of precedent in America for such types of organizations—there were a number of committees with rotating memberships which served to do the work of economic development. There were committees for building, for industrial development, finance, site development, and publicity. Nicely reticulated, each committee was headed by a member of the executive committee.

CAN DO had great organizational strength and esprit. It manipulated associations and swayed public opinion successfully within the Hazleton region. And it convinced outside corporations to invest in Hazleton. I see CAN DO as a controlling mechanism in the regional political economy machine—what might well be identified as the dominance of capital at the most local of local levels.

CAN DO used its semi-skilled labor force as bait to attract companies into locating in Hazleton. It was not lost on Chamber members or CAN DO officials that Hazleton was close to the markets of megalopolis which the interstate system brought temporally closer. Indeed, it was the lobbying efforts of CAN DO influentials and their networks in government that persuaded the federal and state departments of transportation to locate the highways and an interchange between two of them in southern Luzerne County. Obviously location, once the roads were built, became a most important selling point for the CAN DO group.

The contrasts between the pre-capitalist *hustle* and the middle class intercorporate exchanges are not by any means limited to money as the defining medium of the transaction. For the middle class, mainly retail exchanges, there is often a written contract which even when not mentioned looms in back of the verbal one. To the white middle class there is always a third party to economic encounters: the apparatus of the law. Boycie had no legal system to mediate the grievances that arose between unsatisfied persons. There is another distinctive difference as well. In the middle class system, the goods and the payment do not create credit between the parties. You are supposed to deliver the goods promised and pay the full amount for the goods received. By and large this is the way the bulk of transacting is done. If this does not go according to the norms, an unsatisfied person may legitimately seek redress through the courts. It is as if the *hustle* bonds persons, while the retail transaction moves goods and services between legally defined social actors.

* * *

As far as I could tell CAN DO operated the way business elites in other American cities have been observed to do, for it was the only form of social organization that could culturally cut across the community to organize it to achieve economic goals, indeed communal goals (keeping the children around), due to divisiveness of the churches and synagogues and the diversity of cultural-national heritages. A protestant minister could not have, in the name of his particular church, organized the community, a union leader could not have formed a communitarian movement in the name of the union. In America the central government does not systematically undertake to address the social needs of depressed areas through established administrative means. There was no overarching ideology that could have galvanized everyone. Only some social form, such as a corporation, could have utilized the resources of other corporate entities to achieve its ends. The only basis I could find for integration was a corporation, one that persuaded through the media in a well-organized campaign, and that used communal symbols to make a believable promise to the local people that there might well be the opportunity to labor. Organization at the community level was accomplished by intercorporate coalitions formed through networks of influence by a centralized coordinating nonsectarian, nonprofit incorporated company.

Ethnographers who begin to canvass a region almost invariably attempt to construct the world from the ground up. Indeed the modern ethnography of Malinowski was developed and conducted out of doors in uncarpentered societies at the most local level. Ethnography in America for the most part has to be conducted indoors, as it also is done in village societies, inside private domestic or company buildings. Moving the method from outdoors to indoors makes for some major adjustments, particularly in accessibility. Built worlds are less socially and physically available than ones occurring in open communal space. Our hosts in Hazleton, the business people active in community promotion, hosted cocktail parties for us with the people who became our informants. Through sociable means we were able to move rather easily from company to company and government office to government office. We did not restrict ourselves to the Chamber's business community, however, and went from shop to shop and door to door where we could. Indeed, Berger and I drove every road that the Jeep could navigate, including infrequently used pathways through the corporation-abandoned coalfields. We photographed and sketched, drew house-types and settlement patterns, and keyed the visual materials to topographic maps and our field notebooks. I summarized our spatial generalizations in a scratch atlas, sketches of regional spatial arrays of social and cultural life. We interviewed shopkeepers, people working on their properties, bankers, real estate agents, farmers, retirees, widowed women who had been married to miners, former miners suffering from black lung disease, mine owners, doctors, lawyers, seismologists, union leaders, clergymen—the list goes on and on.

During several interviews Berger or I would say that we were writing a book on the region. This strategy led to problems of people wanting a copy and having to worry about promising a book in exchange for the information we were seeking. On one occasion in a small town we split up and Berger took the grocery store and post office as his place to interview and I went to another business establishment. I said in advance, "Let's don't say we're writing a book anymore, it's leading to too many problems." Berger agreed. When we left the hamlet, we were followed by a man in a pickup truck who shadowed us—we hoped it was not ominous—as we drove to the next small town. We pulled onto a side street and he pulled in behind us. The wind was coldly blowing but he got out and came over to the driver's side. The first words out of his mouth were, "I heard you were writing a book . . . " *Oh no*, I thought, *Berger told people back there we were writing a book.* As the man stood there, Berger proceeded to interview him across my lap in the freezing breeze, the plastic window of my Jeep unzipped for our conversation. The man told us his grandmother would surely be interested in talking with us about her perceptions of the history of the region. She was old, he said, and lived with him and his wife and their small son. They were caring for her and she was in exchange leaving the house to them. They were a working class family and we made an appointment then to talk with him and his wife and his grandmother. It proved to be a valuable experience. We talked with them all at length and I climbed the mountain with his younger brother to survey the working class usufruct of high altitudes, especially in regard to deer hunting. We were able to trace this and other blue collar families by taking their oral histories. We gained about a hundred year time-depth in this manner. People had moved extensively from the 1870s to the 1970s in search of work particularly in the mines and on the railroads.

CAN DO, we discovered, was among the coalfield community groups especially successful as a competitor for federal dollars. In its industrial park strategy CAN DO was extremely successful—its parks were fully leased in 1974. That same year, CAN DO claimed a nearly full regional employment. The men who engineered the success traveled to other American communities and to European cities to tell their story.

CAN DO had a profound effect on the local landscape. Mined lands were reclaimed for an industrial park which was provided with the services of sewers and water. A by-pass was built around the city at CAN DO's expense. The largest impact which resembled the complex of forces at work in the megalopolitan corridor was the suburbanization of the agricultural Conyngham valley seven miles north of the city, the results of which left downtown Hazleton looking deserted, its shops for rent or sale. Agriculture declined as a result of increased land prices, older residents on fixed incomes were hurt by the rise in property taxes, and the remaining farmers, recently engaged in dairying, became disconnected from the local economy and joined the Philadelphia milkshed. The schools of the mountain and the valley were consolidated and the effect on the local communities was felt as their children were bused to large, distant, and impersonal schools.

From the traditional ground up approach, the studying up method of anthropologists in America, much remained mysterious to me. I could not figure out how the country was run by staying on the ground level in examining Hazleton. It was as if I were catching glimpses. What I only partially understood was how the country operated on the regional level and above. Two things finally became apparent: one, that these small corporate structures like CAN DO existed all over in many cities of the country and were, therefore, identical and numerous social formations; and two, that a similar set of principles operated from the most poorly ordered grouping in some community groping to stave off a highway sited through their town, up to the national level polity which operated according to the same principles of incorporation and influence.

Toward the end of the field investigation in the late 1970s I went to visit the executives of the large service corporations, the electrical power and telephone companies. I had heard in interviews how important the large regional utilities were as stimuli for development in northeastern Pennsylvania. I believed I had to understand the large-scale service companies and supralocal positions they held in relation to the local community.

What I began to discern was an altitude far above the locality. The big regional companies were composed of tightly ordered social forms with a presence at the national level. The major corporate players shared common and competing interests and practices and resembled one another. It was they who helped make this so-called life on the ground that ethnographers study a possibility. A hierarchy of institutional forms rose out of sight to the ordinary citizen of the country. Indeed, if there was a punchline at the close of the research, it came as the surprise that the large service corporations bought land that helped the CAN DO membership successfully develop their industrial parks and bring something close to full employment to the region by 1974. More important than the particular site for land development was the management expertise for economic growth that the large companies brought to the coalfield communities. It was they who suggested and helped set up the CAN DO and CAN DO-like not-for-profit corporations in the cities of the anthracite coalfields. The large firms also required their regional vice-presidents take a residence in such places as Hazleton and other key cities in order to help shape growth. For the large companies who vended services, the interests of CAN DO and their own were identical, like mirrors of one another but at different scales. Both the large region-wide companies and the small cities with their professionals and business members needed consumers; and economic development—that complex of infrastructure, public finance, pork barrel, and private corporate initiative—had to be coalesced through a kind of cooperative lobbying and entrepreneurship in order to attract customers.

At another conceptual level, I found in the culture of the region a continuous onslaught of instability and change, re-formation, tied directly and indirectly to the world economy. Capitalism despite the stability of social form in the capitalist firm, no matter which sector, and with its particular form of government, behaves as a wildly fluctuating social order and certainly destabilizes localities. As Marx passionately announced in the *Manifesto*, capitalism transforms the entire planet, but this transformation is painfully felt at the specific town or small city level. In these places, capitalist social forms continually re-create themselves in order to respond to the destablilization of privately as well as publicly induced economic and social transformations.

This was not the America of the conservative social theorists, of Durkheim, Weber, or Parsons. Nor did this America belong to the world that anthropologists tended to impute to the remnants of smaller-scale societies far from the cities of our country. Nor was it something in between. Rather, this discovery was something alongside the theories of sociologists and the usual findings of anthropologists.

With a sense of the history of an energy shift from coal to oil and its immediate impact on the hard coal country, I can say that I had become aware of a nonfunctionalist social order, far from equilibrium, that at seemed to be only temporarily stable at best. Functionalist models of social organization, whether anthropological or sociological, seemed wide of the empirical mark.

The sense of discovery seemed to be like a climb upward and outward from the Philadelphia ghetto field experience. A spatial sense of opening, increased scale, and poorly defined but real-feeling hierarchy attended the research in Hazleton on the mountain and in the valley. In addition to the laminations of hierarchy, there was the discovery of fluctuations and instabilities that seemed wholly interior to the system.[4] Looking back, I see that the urban businessmen and professionals in southern Luzerne County recolonized the regional resources that had been left nearly useless in the aftermath of the breakup of the banking-rail-mining interests.

4. In a paper marked by unusual intelligence and that puts together human cultural evolution with Prigoginian instabilities and identifies the international role of corporate management, see Taylor who concludes that his model "evokes the broad sweep of human evolution because managers operate in a global economy which unites the First, Second, and Third World economies, transcends political, social and cultural differences and interacts on one level or another with every business, public institution and managed system on earth. These systems are linked cultural entities whose collective evolution drives human cultural evolution.

"Involving changes in technology, behaviour, aesthetics, organzational design, corporate cultures and value systems, cultural evolution encompasses purposeful development and coherence as well as chaotic and accidental change at bifurcation points. The view of management as an effective agent of cultural evolution sees an open system, fluctuating, irreversibly changing, operating far-from-equilibrium and inevitably involving the emergence of the novel. This view involves a dual role for management: both as a culture among other evolving cultures and at the same time a culture which is capable of consciously impacting the process of change itself.

"Bifurcation points in cultural evolution appear with accelerating frequency." And he ends on what may be a bit of an overly-optimistic note explaining that "it is this possibility of purposeful intervention in the processes of cultural evolution that may offer hope and insight as we attempt to manage in an increasingly complex and rapidly evolving environment." Lauren Taylor, "Management: Agent of Human Cultural Evolution," *Futures* (October 1987):526.

5
Nonprofit
Entrepreneur

The Doe Run team plays the Adidas team on the field of the Brandywine Polo Club. Photo by Benjamin Miller.

We were through talking and I stood up to leave, the workday was over. Frolic Weymouth pushed the chair away from his desk and asked if I had to be anywhere just then. I said no and he invited me to his house to ride with him in his coach-and-four. As he stood and stretched I noticed that he wore the usual gear of a polo player, inexpensive white Levi corduroys, a pair of cowboy boots, and a dress shirt open at the collar. We left the small office building of the Brandywine River Conservancy, an organization that he had founded in 1967, and we drove to his house a couple of miles away, just north of the Delaware border in southern Pennsylvania. He parked his car in the courtyard between the barn and the house; he opened the rear hatch and pulled out some rose bushes he had purchased at a reduced rate from a local nurseryman. For a few minutes we walked around the yard and he asked my advice on where he ought to place them. I lowered my voice just a little and acted authoritative in suggesting where they ought to go.

We turned to the sound of the hooves of the horses on the granite cobble driveway of the courtyard and walked from the lawn toward the barn. There were three grooms—two young women and a young man. The man had what I thought was an English accent and a drooping eyelid and seemed either diffident or world-weary. The women were much less alienated from the work. One stood holding the reins next to the front two horses. Frolic explained that two of the four horses were new and he wanted to judge how they performed. Frolic asked me to sit with him on the driver's bench. Another man, older, an equestrian photographer, climbed up and sat in the middle seat on the roof. One of the women handed the reins to Frolic, he spread the blanket over our laps and turned to me and remarked that the New York custom-made coach was a Brewster; it was built in the nineteenth century.

It was handsome, lacquered in a gunboat gray trimmed in maroon.

He guided the quartet of standardbreds up a rise in back of the house and he asked me if I would like a drink. One of the grooms handed me a gin and tonic. As we gained the top of the hill, I could see in every direction Frolic's estate. His land resembled nothing so much as the eighteenth-century rural English countryside. There were no other houses in sight. I listened as he recounted how he and England's Prince Philip had urged the International Olympic Committee to add coach-and-four racing as a competitive event.

From 1975 through 1978 I lived in southern Chester Country, Pennsylvania, most of that time in the Brandywine River watershed. I conducted ethnography among the agriculturalists, suburbanites, and estate owners of the regional Philadelphia and Wilmington upper class.

His mother a du Pont and one of the heiresses of that family fortune,

Frolic Weymouth had played since he was eighteen in the Brandywine Polo Club and had later formed the Brandywine River Conservancy and Museum. The Museum was dedicated to the art of Andrew Wyeth and the Brandywine School of illustrators. Wyeth lived just a few miles up the river. Frolic had become friends with him, married one of his nieces, and done a senior project on a Wyeth painting his last year at Yale.

I came away from the late afternoon ride with Frolic with a sense of the private landscape based on personal ownership by the very rich, a self conscious world of exclusiveness, views and the aesthetics of well thought out design.

* * *

Boycie and Frolic lived forty kilometers from one another, a day's walk, an hour by car. I imagine that I can have these two meet in the world just as they inhabit the simultaneous space of my mind, just as they are both contemporary Americans. I would like to take them and fold the distance between them on the line midway between the two points until they touch face-to-face:

Boycie ———————————— | ———————————— Frolic

bend the distance in half and create a revery as to how they might meet. *Boycie and Frolic bump into one another in the South Philadelphia Italian Market. Boycie averts his eyes but says nothing. Frolic begins to comment but thinks better of it.*

No that cannot happen. Frolic has not been to the Italian Market since childhood.

Boycie becomes a groom and works for Frolic. He hitches the horse for an evening ride and serves drinks to those riding on the front bench.

No that cannot happen either. Boycie has had nothing to do with horses and had not prepared himself for personal service, and does not leave a ten square block area of South Philly. The bucolic Chester County countryside would have no meaning for him, no resonance in his aesthetic of performance and rough theater. He is too profane to work for someone like Frolic. He would not put up with the demeaning nature of waiting on someone.

Frolic panhandles for quarters in the shadow of Martin Luther King, Jr., Plaza. Boycie is a member of one of the richest families in the country. . . .

America.

Where forty kilometers can take you from some of the poorest, most

3. Andrew Wyeth, *Soaring*, 1950, tempera on masonite. Courtesy of the Shelburne Museum, Shelburne, Vermont.

meager physical surroundings with the least affluence, with the extreme scarcities of quarters or even bedclothes, plumbing, electricity, phones, to a member of one of the richest families on earth.

It staggers the imagination. Folded onto one another, Boycie and Frolic: it damages the sense of reality, what remains of it, to the cynical ethnographer of our incommensurable American differences. I try to understand, to imagine what this means. What, if they met, would they say to one another? We gloss over these essential dissimilarities by clinging to the beliefs that we can all succeed and that our institutions address these disparities.

Frolic's brother lived in the estate area of Chester County and was devoted to the culture of the horse. One year he hosted a national steeplechase event on his property. Frolic's grounds were closer to the familial du Pont chateaus of northern Delaware along the Brandywine, and his brother's were in the West Marlboro township of southern Chester County, Pennsylvania. Both estates were in the Brandywine River watershed and connected in the minds of real estate agents, developers and eager suburbanites by the Chadds Ford-Unionville School District.

Between and around the estates of the du Ponts to the south and West Marlboro Township to the west and north, dairy and beef farms, commercial orchards, and mushroom and cut flower growing defined the economy of the region. The area had been settled by the English Quakers in the seventeenth and eighteenth centuries. The landscape continued to resemble an English rural region. Andrew Wyeth's paintings of Chadds Ford captured the look of the land as it had been implicitly designed by the work of nineteenth- and twentieth-century Quaker farmers.

Wyeth's paintings apparently captured something of the old Quaker agricultural setting (Figure 3). The publicity from the Shelburne Museum which owns Wyeth's *Soaring* contained this quote from him: "One painting I did . . . was a pair of turkey vultures. I was looking down on them from above the fields of a farm far below. As kid I used to lie on my back in the fields in March and April, when you get those turkey vultures here, and find myself looking up and wondering how it would look looking down. I did the painting long before I went up in a plane." This painting has a double resonance. It resembles the poetic imagery in William Carlos Williams's *The Wanderer*, and it foretells the later visual rhetoric of the Brandywine River Museum and Conservancy. In the ideal landscape of the Conservancy, one house would exist in a space with no other residences in sight, and indeed, the effort is made to achieve that effect. With the numerous Wyeth paintings hanging in the Brandywine Museum, the local landscape imagery correlates nicely with the legal efforts of the Environmental Management Center

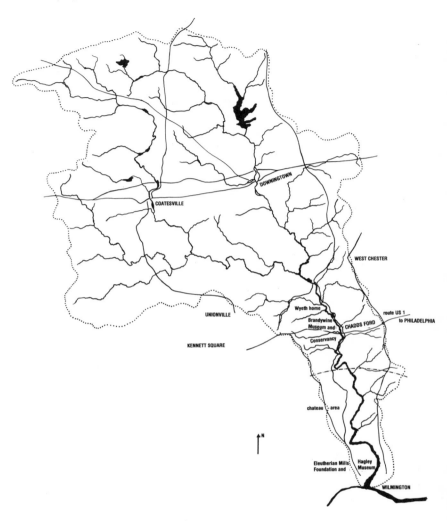

4. The Brandywine River Watershed.

of the Conservancy to realize just that relatively empty agrarian visual prospect.

What indeed had happened to the region, even as Wyeth was painting it, was the result of a double impetus to suburbanize. Both Wilmington and King of Prussia, which is north of Philadelphia, were expanding into the

agrarian lands with great demand for farmland to convert to office buildings and suburban housing. A local businessman who owned property in
Chadds Ford, notably a lumber company in an old mill which no longer
serviced the declining agricultural hinterland, wanted to sell his holdings for
the express purpose of siting a new industry. A commercial sale as opposed
to a residential one would help him realize the greatest dollar value for his
mill and its surrounding acreage.

In founding a museum devoted to the art of Andrew Wyeth and a
conservancy aimed to protect the landscape, there is a dramatic story, for
the water of the Brandywine, as it flowed from Pennsylvania at Chadds Ford
south into northern Delaware passed directly through the du Pont estates,
sacralized home of du Ponts since the early nineteenth century, then by the
DuPont Research and Development facilities, and then into Wilmington
where it served as the central source of water supply for the city, a city
which housed the headquarters of the E. I. DuPont de Nemours and Company. Obviously the stage was set for some sort of upstream intervention by
downstream interests (Figure 4). In this intervention it would seem that we
have revealed the American approach to the landscape, at least in one of its
manifestations, for there was no war waged by armed camps for property or
water. Indeed, the strategy was to resettle the land and redesign the landscape by means of nonprofit institutions. As the water of the Brandywine
flowed out of Pennsylvania and into Delaware, many of those concerned
were connected either as members of a powerful family, or as members of
one of the world's largest industrial firms, or as members of both company
and family.

With the continuous pressure for suburbanization, made up of road
building, bank mortgages, real estate firms, developers and custom home
builders, and with an aging Quaker community which could no longer via-
bly farm and whose sons were marrying du Pont and other suburban
women, there was every opportunity and, indeed from a du Pont point of
view, every necessity to step in and shape growth and development. More
was at stake than the water of the Brandywine River, though that was a
central cultural feature of their regional political economy.

In brief, Frolic volunteered himself and raised funds to buy land and
the old mill in Chadds Ford. He established a Wyeth museum in the mill
and a nature conservancy; he incorporated them into a single institutional
form, a not-for-profit, educational complex, in order to begin to stifle one
branch of growth (the suburban industrial), in favor of another (the residential). Both CAN DO and Frolic used the not-for-profit mode of incorporation
to help them realize their ends. In far-reaching action, Frolic as an entrepreneur of the nonprofit sector put in place an institutional structure that

served to stop the encroachment of industry and that created a highly prized cultural organization used to socialize new suburbanites to the older landscape of estates and farms and to the contemporary cultural values represented by open fields with horses and gracious visual prospects. He set up the means to colonize upstream lands and the consciousness of persons moving to the area for the new cul de sac housing developments that began to replace the fields of the Quaker dairy farmers and horticulturalists.

* * *

If poets were architects they would write manifestos.

Poets are not architects, and tend not to author manifestos but to write poems relatively early in their careers which establish a poetic landscape over which they cross and recross and which becomes the plenum for their subsequent poetic careers. In Western thought it is as if we need specific conceptual terrains on which to work, like military men or geographers, in order to play out our thought or the poetic imagination. Cities. Countrysides. Suburbs.

Here I detour to read for my particular purposes poetic works by William Carlos Williams and Wallace Stevens, both of whom are associated with the landscape near where I am now writing. I use poems of theirs to help mark out the significance of my ethnographic inquiry. Through their writings I make the effort to establish the aims of my own work. Through them I want to resonate with the poetic and ethnographic search for America, an America no longer in discourse with Europe as at the turn of the twentieth century. We now tend to identify ourselves within our own landscape, less so in opposition to European ones.

Williams, who was reared in Rutherford, New Jersey, just across the Hudson River from New York City, attended the University of Pennsylvania in Philadelphia. He was a medical student there at the same time as Ezra Pound. Pound grew up in suburban Philadelphia and the two of them formed a lifelong friendship while at college. Wallace Stevens grew up in Reading, Pennsylvania, then left to attend college at Harvard, moved to New York City and earned a law degree, joined the insurance industry and finally settled permanently in Hartford, Connecticut. Both Williams and Stevens worked and wrote; neither supported themselves by writing or teaching.

Although the presence of Walt Whitman across the river from Philadelphia in Camden continues to enliven conversation and family memories for people in the region, I have chosen Williams and Stevens because they actively searched for an American landscape, because they are moderns, because they are associated with this mid-Atlantic region, because they existed within a culture of private enterprise and because they explored profoundly contrasting poetic landscapes. Their poetic geographies secured a kind of floor plan for their subsequent writing.

Their search can be found in their relatively early poems: Williams wrote *The Wanderer: A Rococo Study,* when he was about thirty years old. Stevens drafted *The Comedian as the Letter C* when he was in his early forties, before the publication of his first book. *The Wanderer* is a poem of placement, the rediscovery of an intimate, well-known place, while *The Comedian* is a work of displacement and recounts a poetic escape from Europe as a sea crossing in search of America. Ethnographers of this country can benefit from both poets. Williams and Stevens were each looking for a landscape whose amplitude was adequate to their imaginative development, a space onto which they could inscribe their sensibilities with words, and a fiction-alizable domain from which they could draw continuously for what we can only call inspiration or emotional energy.

Both poets established powerful attitudes toward the geography of America. I want to discuss the two poems briefly because they set the tone for the inquiry into America that this book documents and at the same time questions.

* * *

As Williams's Wanderer[1] in the opening lines left the woods, an obvious natural setting, he met up with and was guided by a creature who transformed herself from a young crow as she appeared at first, then to a gull, to a woman, and, as the poem progressed, was revealed, finally, as an old queen. With her Williams mapped the urbanscape and so fixed the geography of his poetic future.

The poem is cast as a rite of passage, with all the qualities of a progression in time and rituals of realization and responsibilities that attend the transformation of the child into the adult. For the Wanderer, the rite of passage begins with an advent as he crosses on a ferry toward Manhattan. The city rises in front of him and he addresses the now famous question put to him by the young crow, a question Williams spent his poetic career answering: "How shall I be a mirror to this modernity?"

In the city itself, the Wanderer's transmogrifying muse, now a gull, flies them over Broadway and he sees the anonymous crowds. Airborne again, they sail over another urban area, this time closer to home, Paterson, New Jersey, third largest city in the state, America's first planned industrial urban place. There he witnesses one of those brutal turn-of-the-century labor

1. William Carlos Williams, *The Collected Poems of William Carlos Williams, 1909–1939* Vol.1. A. Walton Litz and Christopher MacGowan, eds. (New York: New Directions, 1986), pp.27–36.

disputes. High above the urban, ethnic working-class, and remote from the experience, Williams nevertheless could write, "It sank deep into the blood . . ." a prefigured image of the Wanderer's final baptism scene in the polluted Passaic River at the close of the poem.

The queen as obese dilapidated muse, again airborne, takes him abroad, but abroad does not convey the aura of European travel and adventure, indeed, it is the New Jersey countryside to which he is flown.

The Wanderer, again from the vantage of a bird's eye view (and this before citizens had access to commercial flights), revisits the scenes of childhood and apparently he now decides to capture poetically the city and export the verse to the reader in the countryside.

In the final section, "Saint James' Grove," the old queen, as he still refers to his battered muse, offers him up to the filthy Passaic River where he is confronted with both past and future. In a graphic scene he is baptised in the industrially soiled water, and he exclaims, "this was me now," a fusion of self and industrial effluent—a marked marriage between the old muse and the river, between the city as culture and the river as violated nature. He, Williams, was to be the poet of this ravaged landscape, flown in imagination over it from the air, and now an interior part of it because he had ritually experienced it as a form of rebirth in its nastiness by means of a total immersion.

The identity of the poet and the specific place—we can find it on the map, drive there in a car—were fused. Williams became the poet of a fixed location and established for himself the urban landscape from which he drew artistic nurturance. As he explained in his *Autobiography*, "I wanted . . . to write about the people close to me: to know in detail, minutely what I was talking about—to the whites of their eyes, to their very smells."[2] As an obstetrician, pediatrician, and poet, he accomplished just that. He invented an America, but through the specificity of a given, tightly embraced point-on-the-map locale.

* * *

Stevens, in his poem, *The Comedian as the Letter C,* scripted himself into the third person as a poetic pilgrim, Crispin.[3] The character Crispin is named after the third century Christian missionary to France who was martyred. Stevens resurrects the martyr as the poet himself who must face potential slaughter by the real claims of domestic life and the workaday world.

Williams's *Wanderer* is a poem of passage, of coming of age, of elemen-

---

2. William Carlos Williams, *The Autobiography of William Carlos Williams* (New York: New Directions, 1967).

3. Wallace Stevens, *The Collected Poems* (New York: Vintage, 1982), pp.27−46.

tal union, discovery, and emplacement. Stevens's poem also establishes a landscape of the imagination but reflects more personal, less social contradictions. It takes the reader on a long tour de force of artistic resignation. Stevens reluctantly resigned himself to the split between the life of the poet and that of the insurance claims attorney who inhabits the mundane, married world. By mapping out a double landscape of north and south, Stevens not so much discovered a reconciliation to his complex situation, but instead found the psychic resources inherent in a shifting movement from one region of the country to another. Such motion served to increase the geographic scope and thus the contrastive richness of his imaginative possibilities.

Crispin the poet set out to sea from Bordeaux to effect a sea change in himself. The *Comedian* served to document a finding of the New World, a sufficient landscape for the young poet. His itinerary took him to Yucatan, from there to Havana, and then to the Carolinas. In the Carolinas, Stevens wrote, Crispin founded a colony. Here Stevens, as he always did, took his own life and aggrandized an aspect of it, in order to better deal with it. This was a movement of the mind that reverses the way most people operate. In a crisis people tend to minimize it and to quickly reestablish the most mundane in order to continue life as usual. Stevens felt he had to resign himself to his domestic situation which was frought from its inception—his father refused to accept his choice of woman to marry. He broke with his father and they never reconciled before the man died. Family as a notion, as something to which Stevens had now committed himself by marriage, in the *Comedian* expanded to become a colony.

Stevens, in his discovery of America, arranged for himself an expanded landscape, the colorful, noisy, tropical abundance and *the polar-purple*, as he called it, of North America. His colony as larger-than-life family he founded in the Carolinas, full of contradictions; it was inhabited first by a hermit and it was not terribly north at all. The Carolinas themselves were first colonized by the English as a zone for tropical agriculture. Hermits typically don't found or live in colonies.

For Williams the aesthetic world was set in a dirty industrial city full of immigrants and new electrically powered machines. His artistic motion telescoped in and out: he zoomed for close ups, delivered a Polish immigrant woman's baby, and zoomed back out again. From a moment's distant privacy he wrote a poem and thereby refreshed himself. His own cultural distance as a middle class or upper middle class professional played endlessly against a physician's momentary physical contact with a patient; it was this poetic remoteness slammed against the intimate scale and back out that marked Williams's relationship to the poetic landscape.

Stevens invented the New World as a large island of oppositions of heat and cold, fantastic flourescence of vegetation and animal life placed against the simiplifications of winter and snow. He moved the external world into the imaginative world and by the medium of verse ejected the poetically transformed landscape back into the world. There was no fusion for Stevens, either of his opposed landscapes or of his insurance occupation with his poetics, or of his domestic life with his artistic efforts. There was no baptism in the filth of the industrial river, no zooming close and out again. Rather, Stevens crossed and recrossed a temperate and tropical America of purple moonlight and golden, sapping sunlight, resigned but unreconciled. His landscapes were aesthetic arrangements of mainly domesticated natural elements—cabbages, dogwoods, magnolias, roses, melons, peaches, plums, figs, or yarrow—and imaginative contact between them and himself as poet. It was a large, but circumscribed geography that he desired, a great land mass, on which he remained forever restless, forever playing his imagination over, as he lived his life and as he drew what he felt he needed from its atmosphere and its various foliage.

Stevens's dual landscape of north and south and Williams's industrial urban life were the physical settings of private enterprise. Williams was shaped by the great and bitter strike in Paterson that pitted corporate ownership against the working man. Stevens reached for the image of a colony as his destination and challenge to form in the New World. Above all the colony in British North America was initially a private corporate form, one of the central cultural elements in the formation of American life.

The poetic search for America, represented by Williams and Stevens, is not a search restricted by any means to them, for it includes other poets and generations of fiction writers. In the desire to create an American landscape of imaginative resource, Williams, Stevens, and others are personally involved; the search for landscape is coupled with the search for the American self. Self and location become fused in Williams, endlessly prowled by Stevens. Ethnographers can draw from both the movement of fusion and restless movement in their inquisitive relations with American culture.

The relatively rapid telescoping inward to study Hazleton, then the more languid roving over the Chester County landscape during the last twelve years, suggest first Williams with his overview and close-up, and then Stevens with his resolute motion over a large expanse without achieving a final completion. These modes of relation between poet and place bear an internal relation with ethnographers who employ similar kinds of embrace and peripatetics.

In a sense, Crispin was Stevens the poet, in his act of discovering and founding a colony. Frolic Weymouth, too, was a shaper, by managing an upstream landscape. The ethnographer as well, engages in discovery, to acquire and disseminate new knowledge. Poet, entrepreneur, and ethnographer overlay one another. Each engages in the appropriation of territory whether aesthetic, physical, or conceptual.

* * *

Stevens's *Comedian* rewrites the mythic discovery of America that began with the actual colonization of Virginia, for the land was first amazingly sensed by smell by the sensual Elizabethans, days before the high ground was sighted! The legendary taking of the country, treated often enough in American literature, is central to the ethnographic inquiry sketched on these pages. For Stevens as for others, the discovery is made by an individual, and like others, the new found world is a land already inhabited.

During a thunderstorm in the Yucatan Crispin's mind "was free"

And more than free, elate, intent, profound . . .

That was not in him in the crusty town
From which he sailed.

The mythic proportions of the poetic hero setting up in an America which sustains a myth of freedom can be juxtaposed with the absence of aesthetic treatment of corporate form I have just mentioned. Crispin's pilgrimage was not that of a bloody fortune-seeking conqueror, but of a man who, with deep ambivalence, set up house and tried to convince himself that despite the demands of domestic life which drains the energy of both philosophers and poets he would find that

For all it takes it gives a humped return
Exchequering from piebald fiscs unkeyed.

He tells himself that the royal treasury of everyday life will be unlocked by wife and children, the daughters with curls.

On the professional level, my search has not been conducted for reconciliation or lack thereof between the imagination and everyday life. I have wanted to find out what it is in this country that organizes us, or to put it more actively, what cultural inventions we have unconsciously evolved to make our lives and our landscapes what we experience when we walk out the door or drive across the country. The house and yard connected to other houses and yards, to corporate and industrial settings, commercial strips, the cultural landscape.

Anglo-Americans, though the practices are now widespread in the culture, unceasingly organize themselves in quite particular ways to achieve specific ends, that is, to effect changes. As unremarkable as the formulation sounds, the abstract statement of the activities of organization, which remain largely out of consciousness and are by no means central to scholarly inquiry, identifies the very cultural formations that underlie the way we live in this country. The corporation is, whatever else it is, a colonizing form. The reason we organize ourselves is to transform something—things, events, ideas and people—whether our property, our settlements, our natural environments or our neighbor's opinions. The culture of capitalism through a pragmatic social form achieves and reveals itself in a cultural mode of continuous colonization, most of it internal to the country, much of it external.

My myth of discovery joins all the others and fits almost invisibly within those other genres of self-exploration that seem so necessary to our polyglot collective consciousness. It is not the European escape and American discovery by Crispin, not a resignation or reconciliation story, or the poetics of fusion between self and urban place, but an exploration driven by estrangement and for a way to think about how we experience ourselves and what we do. At the same time there is something like Crispin's voyage here, for it was motivated as a personal odyssey into the self that culture built and into the culture that our selves have made.

One of the puzzles of America and of special interest to anthropologists resides in the never-solved issues of our singleness as a nation and our joined-while-separate complex patchwork of national and religious cultural streams. Is not the unity and diversity of humanity one of the great humanistic themes, comparable to that of nature and culture? It was once addressed by anthropologists in the early modern period in such works as Frazer's *The Golden Bough*, though now out of style.

Frolic was like Crispin but not in motion toward a resignation. Indeed, just the opposite. In the section of *Comedian*, "The Idea of a Colony," Stevens begins the section

> Nota: his soil is man's intelligence.
> That's better. That's worth crossing seas to find.
> Crispin in one laconic phrase laid bare
> His cloudy drift and planned a colony.

For as Stevens uses the imagination as metaphysic in his poem, it is above all that metaphysic of larger-than-life magnitudes, it is the continuous transformation through scale of the smallness of the ordinary. Frolic accomplished something like the same thing: he colonized an extensive landscape larger than his own estate by capitalist means, not through the poetic, but rather through the practical imagination. I tell what amounts to a sketch of his story which extends to the similar-while-different work of the men of CAN DO. Our social forms are meant to continuously reshape our lives.

The internal colonization of the Brandywine watershed was accomplished through the nature conservancy, now called the Brandywine River Conservancy, through its Environmental Management Center. The staff of the Conservancy worked through the local townships in the public sector to help write ordinances for them and aided the large landowners in the private sector to acquire easements on their land. For the individual landowner, easements restricted future development on their property. Easements served as a charitable contribution and a tax deduction because the development rights had been donated to a nonprofit educational or charitable institution. Much land was given outright to the Conservancy, which it then managed as a public trust and yet as its own property.

As in the classical capitalist activities in the Anglo-American world, an institutional framework was legally incorporated to manage the course of economic development for its own ends. In the case of the Conservancy, the ends of the company were carefully laminated onto the growing environmental sensitivities of the increasingly affluent suburbanites. A clean Brandywine became the first rallying focus. The Conservancy used sophisticated scientific knowledge of hydrology and limnology. These branches of science were employed as a rhetoric of persuasion for the suburbanite constituency in the legal discourse of township zoning and Pennsylvania highway development, two engines of residential growth at the suburban-rural fringe. Coupled with the rhetoric of science in the Conservancy was the ideology of relatively empty social space inhabited by a single residential structure as in the landscapes Wyeth painted. The Brandywine River Museum, itself a suburban agency, fixed the Wyeth look of the land in intimate connection to its sister organization, the Conservancy, which had mastered the legal mechanisms to achieve that look.

Museum and Conservancy as legally incorporated entities not only appealed to a strong and growing local constituency but drew for their board members from a national and regional elite. The wife of a former President of the United States served on the board, as did several governors of Pennsylvania and Delaware. I could trace the relationships of region and country linked through influential persons, though not directly to the national congress or judiciary. Connections to Congress and the federal court system were prominently made in other portions of southern Chester County and northern Delaware.

Eight years after Frolic began his Museum and Conservancy I was living on a dairy farm with a family whose ancestors had homesteaded Chester

County under William Penn's colonial proprietorship. I received a grant to study the mushroom industry while I was also examining the dairy operations, and so focused on agribusiness in the region, of which the estates and the culture of the horse were an elite aspect. One of the owners of an extensive mushroom business, for example, played polo in the Brandywine Polo Club and one of his sons was a top-seeded young international player. Both the dairy industry and the mushroom industry were linked from the local landscape to the national congressional and administrative levels, and this relationship was established locally—as well as all across the country, for it is how we as a nation are in part organized—through trade associations.

The dairy industry reaches from the local farmstead in say Wisconsin or Chester County, Pennsylvania, upward through its dairy cooperatives, to the national trade associations which are themselves companies. The mushroom industry—and there were two hundred and seventy-five growers in the Kennett Square area, not more than ten miles from Chadds Ford— through its American Mushroom Institute, lobbied in state and federal legislatures for growers' interests and wrote bills to be introduced by lawmakers; it allocated money raised from dues for scientific research and development at state universities on the nutritional aspects of mushrooms and on ways of preserving them for shipping and shelf storage; it marketed mushrooms through food advertising firms located on Madison Avenue; it disseminated information throughout the mushroom growing industry by means of a members' newsletter; and it manipulated the industry's public image by generating information in the form of press releases available to the newspapers, radio and television.

What became apparent was that even the local civic associations were hierarchically ordered from the modest regional chapters up to the national, even the international levels, an example being the local Chamber of Commerce. The landscape, as it was pictured by Wyeth, as it was lived in by dairy farmers and other agriculturalists, and by the suburbanites was a capitalist one from bottom to top. Whether the sectors were for-profit or not-for-profit, they were organized hierarchically and from east to west to colonize space, physical materials, and human activities.

Not only are corporations organized nearly identically (if we take the long view), but the practices of corporate actors, whether nonprofit, for-profit or public, resemble one another profoundly in America. Consider the Tennessee Valley Authority (TVA), which was the most ambitious national-level sponsored public works program in the world in its time. When a new chairman, Marvin T. Runyon, was sworn in, Ronald Smothers,[4] writing for

4. Ronald Smothers, "Auto Executive Ready to Take on the T.V.A.," *New York Times* (24 January 1988).

the *New York Times*, interviewed him. Mr. Runyon told the reporter "T.V.A. was created in the image of a private company and the fact that it had wandered away from that somewhat means that it could possibly wander back." Runyon meant to bring his expertise from running an Asian-based auto manufacturing company in the United States to the challenge of managing the huge nonprofit energy authority.

* * *

There is a magic line running somewhere through the middle of the bourgeoisie which slices it into an upper and a lower half. I am here using spatial imagery to portray the way our country is organized as a stack of not very discrete strata. Within the upper middle class—however that contested idea is defined—there is a threshhold, an above and a below. Below the threshhold are the corporate members and managers who make good salaries. These people experience a horizontal world of others like themselves, and experience a rather short distance between them and those who are below them. They are typified, for my point here, by remaining unaware of the Big Picture, the top down overview that one acquires by inhabiting the apex of the the particular social pyramid wherein one may typically dwell. If I am a middle level manager, things look pretty much as if I am in the middle, there is a lot of corporate structure over my head which remains unclear to me and out of reach, and a fair amount below it, but I do not have a lot of real fiscal or social power.

Above that line, there is a sea change, a quantum leap of some sort. This is the level of vice-presidents and presidents, chairs of boards, executives and highest level managers. From above the magic line, one looks downward and sees a vast array of not only one's own bailiwick, but outward to one's neighbors, to the great community of corporations. One begins to conceptualize corporate America, or the energy sector, or the defense interests of the country, or that relevant segment of the international economy. One has a conception of a large block of some significant and powerful social sector. The inhabitants of this higher level endlessly refine their almost Olympian vantage point. The high view downward resembles Williams's overflight by his gross muse, but without the intimacy of even momentary embrace, the baptism in filth. In part, they cultivate it through continuing effective use of real power which changes the behavior of those below them and effects a transformation of material and capital, what I have been calling, in its broadest sense, colonization. These persons wield significant power and control. For Frolic, due to his wealth and national level connections, there was a broad, top down view of the entire Brandywine River watershed, all two hundred and ninety square miles within Chester County, Pennsylvania, its institutional frameworks, its citizenry and even its potential for subtle uses of existing local values, and equally subtle possibilities for shaping it toward the aesthetic and residential development interests he implicitly held.

* * *

There is another image of America, tied to the capitalist landscapes I have studied. It is of the familiar political shapes in which we live. America is made up of triads. We have three branches of government, the legislative, the administrative, and the judicial. These three divisions are replicated in versions of descending power at three levels of scale, the federal, the state, and the local governments. Another triad, used by the economists, divides our corporations into three sectors. The classification orders the large-scale sectors by their relationship to profits and their provision of types of services. These three sectors, mentioned previously, are termed the *public* which is government, the *private* which is the profit-making corporation, and the *not-for-profit* or nonprofit which includes our poltical parties, trade associations, and civic and voluntary associations. What I would like to emphasize is that from top to bottom all these organizations have the familiar capitalist form of the corporation whether it be the United States Government, General Motors or Exxon (alternately America's largest), or the Rockefeller Foundation.

As a vision of a dynamic society I further have the strong impression that while the people elect their national and state congressmen, the corporations, directly through their companies and indirectly through lobbyists—those often-noted special interests—write or critically monitor and substantively shape the laws of the land or so influence them, that it is our private corporate America that sets the legal and fiscal agenda for public and nonprofit America.[5] This impression derives directly from fieldwork, from

5. National political leaders, whether liberal, conservative, or the noted solid middle, can organize downward and galvanize political action through national and local level voluntary associations. When Reagan was president of the country and negotiated a new treaty on intermediate-range nuclear forces (INF) with Soviet Leader Mikhail Gorbachev, the conservative establishment took full aim to sabotage senate ratification. "In a letter mailed to 110,000 people, John M. Fisher, the 65-year-old chairman of the American Security Council, urged members to barrage the Senate with letters opposing the treaty. Fisher persuaded retired Adm. Thomas Moorer, former Chairman of the Joint Chiefs of Staff, and more than 2,000 other retired admirals and generals to sign a petition opposing any arms agreements that 'would lock' the United States 'into strategic or military inferiority' or 'make our allies more vulnerable, like the proposed INF treaty.' Sixty organizations endorsed the petition, Fisher said, including Citizens for Reagan, the Naval Reserve Association, the Assembly of Captive European Nations, the American Federation of Small Businesses, and the National Confederation of Ethnic Groups." (Hedrick Smith, "The Right Against Reagan," *New York Times Magazine*" [17 January 1988]), p.38.

participating intimately in the workings of local level politics, and through habituating some of the very largest American corporations. As I reread Adam Smith's scathing critique of the pervasive influence of English merchants, I find continuities between the eighteenth century and the twentieth: "Of the greater part of the regulations concerning the colony trade, the merchants who carry it on, it must be observed, are the principal advisers."[6]

From an individual point of view, we live simultaneously in a multitude of companies that have worked out between themselves portions of our lives and identities over which they will exercise limited influence or control. I am employed by one of the two largest nonprofit employers in the City of Philadelphia, the University of Pennsylvania. I pay taxes to the City of Philadelphia, which controls some of the money I make but does not provide direct services to me. I have a residence in Lower Merion Township, Pennsylvania, where I also pay taxes and receive benefits such as schooling, water supply waste and snow removal, fire protection, police protection, and park and recreation facilities. I work in the not-for-profit sector, live in the public sector, but also consult to a private corporation which makes profits by marketing financial services. The primary company for which I work, the University of Pennsylvania, sets law-like rules which enable me to labor outside it one day in seven. I have a contractual relationship with the University and also with the private corporation. The two contracts each account for my membership with the other company. In 1968 there were 1,600,000 private sector, profit making companies in the country by one count.[7] But in 1983, according to the 1987 *Statistical Abstracts of the United States*, there were more than 6,000,000 corporations. That count included mutual organizations such as insurance companies, banks, savings and loans, as well as business trusts and cooperative banks.

My point here is that we all have multiple corporate memberships in which the corporations work out among themselves the kinds of identities and relationships that members can possibly have. My further point is that this is America, that these forms define our lives. These forms have replaced kinship as the foundations of social experience—when this society is compared with the small scale cultural systems usually studied by anthropologists. Beyond form, we must recognize that these corporate structures are designed to engage one another. Indeed, our environmental problems are worked out between nonprofit conservation firms who lobby with governments against private sector corporations. It is as if our companies have

6. Adam Smith, *The Wealth of Nations*. Vol.II (Chicago: University of Chicago Press, 1976), p.96.

7. Shi Chang Wu, "Distribution of Economic Resources in the United States," mimeographed (Chicago: National Opinion Research Center, 1974).

caught us up within their endless contendings with one another for particular corporate advantage, for access to resources and for the determination over allocations of assets whether material or intellectual.

A central feature of the corporate experience, from an individual's perspective and hidden from explicit view to us in everyday life, is a legal or quasi-legal boundary set by the company, a boundary that helps define who we are and what we can do. I say hidden from view because we are all too unconscious of the effects of the in-corporation of our society, indeed, our everyday life, and what it has done to our cultural existence.

One of the effects tends to result in a pacification of spontaneity and the endless structurings of managed relationships between persons. The possible characterological constrictions from living wholly caught up in one large company after another become painfully evident. Consider the following letter. A suburban housewife and mother who graduated from college, earned an MBA degree from the Stanford business school, then moved immediately to a middle-level management position in a big American corporation, writes to one of her friends. Her friend is also a mother with two children. The letter is plaintively eloquent and disheartening.

> I am just beginning to realize how isolated is the life of a mother at home with such young children as mine. I have decided not to return to work before Lee's first birthday, so I am now missing the primary vehicle for social interaction in my life — work (or should I say, my paying job within a large organization). I have always had school or work to provide people to talk to — I've never felt I needed to search for such people. Now that search is one of my primary objectives while at home, partly for myself and partly for Debbie and Lee. I never realized what effort it takes to initiate and to maintain relationships when you don't see people on a day-to-day basis. I find the process doesn't come naturally — I'm always thinking in terms of priority tasks, and it always seems there's something more important to do than socialize. I also realize I'm rather shy — afraid that people won't want me for a friend and so afraid to make that first phone call or impromptu visit. I've tried to overcome these obstacles lately by making a list of all the people with whom I'd like to keep in touch — by phone, letter, or in person. I'm going to keep track of when I communicate with these people and to maintain a minimum standard of periodic contact — such as once a month for some, twice a month for others, etc. It sounds like a cold and overly rational approach to dealing with people, but otherwise I let too much time go by without communicating. At least one friendship has already suffered as a result. . . .

It is difficult to measure the extent of the incorporatedness of our lives and its sway over the national character. My professional associations are incorporated, my various governmental bodies are incorporated, my employers are incorporated. In 1987 it was estimated in the *Encyclopedia of Associations* that there were 20,000 national nonprofit corporations in the United States. This count barely scratches the surface because all the little civic associations, the local garden clubs, the local Italian men's association, and thousands of others from Maine to Hawaii elude precise enumeration. More to the point, if any collection of Americans for any reason want to accomplish some collective action (and they repeatedly do), they create a corporate form of social organization to do just that. These associations colonize in the sense that they are designed for the express purpose of making some sort of directed changes in the members' institutional and cultural environment.

I have just mentioned those corporate forms that encase us within themselves, those more than 6,000,000 corporations, mutual associations, and trusts, that vend us our commodites, whether fetishes or the mere play of simulacra. This morning I walked out of the house and turned left toward the village center. I walked past Mrs. Smith's house, then a vacant lot, and then a dwelling with three apartments made over from the old blacksmith's shop. The next building was the Gulf station that sells gas, located at the intersection that marked one end of the village. The Gulf Oil Corporation in 1984 was headquartered in Pittsburgh and was, according to *Fortune Magazine* of that year, the eleventh largest firm in the country as ranked by sales. On the opposite corner the Sun Corporation, headquartered on Philadelphia's Main Line and ranked in 1987 as twentieth by *Fortune*, had franchised a station to a sole proprietor, a man with whom I have a longstanding joking relationship. Two large nonprofit corporations were represented on the other two corners of the intersection: the Boy Scouts of America and the Catholic Church.[8]

As I walked in the same direction up the street in town the next firm was a wholly owned, cooperatively managed subsidiary of the Atlantic and Pacific (A&P) food stores. There are twenty one retail businesses in town

8. It is well worth noting that American religious institutions from the charismatics through high church are legally incorporated entities. As do nations, they can suffer from constitutional crises. When one pentecostal preacher, the Reverend Jimmy Swaggart of the Assemblies of God, jeapordized his 150-million-dollar-a-year television ministry by repeatedly visiting a prostitute, it fomented a legal crisis between the national denomination and the Louisiana District Council. Reverend Swaggart's lawyer told the *New York Times* (1 March 1988) that "We have an issue involving the constitution and bylaws of this organization." He went on to explain in defense of his client that the conflict was whether the national presbytery or the Louisiana District Council had the right to discipline ministers.

including three hardware stores, two real estate agencies, and a branch of a large regional bank. The Village Store Hardware is an unincorporated sole proprietorship while the Merion Square Hardware is an incorporated firm. I walked into the shops and asked the proprietors a single question: "Are you incorporated?" A strange look invariably passed over the face of the man or woman I asked. Then we launched into talk about business. I want to stress by this example that we not only live framed within complex sets of corporate structures but that our contemporary mode of living demands that other sets of corporate structures (in which others live) vend us all the products we see displayed. As I walked into the pharmacy and asked the head pharmacist, "Are you incorporated?" a salesman from a major pharmaceutical house was taking an order to replace depleted stock. The pharmacy is incorporated and was one company buying from another. Every one of the almost incomprehensible number of items that I saw arrayed at the hardware store, the pharmacy, the supermarket, and the gas station were vended by relatively large corporate players. The messages that assaulted me from the packaging was written inside large incorporated institutions. I was caught up entirely within the play of companies and corporately designed visual and written rhetorics that reached persuasively toward me for my disposable income.

* * *

Cultural historians, literary theorists, anthropologists, political philosophers, social theorists, artists, and others converge in their thought and practice on an incompletely defined place roughly designated *cultural theory*. Cultural theorists desire nothing less than a comprehension of our historical moment, though usually expressed in resistance and critique.

In the seventeenth century, a cultural historian explains, the rapid growth of the impersonal forces of the marketplace began to dislodge Culture from Economy. In Victorian Anglo-America, champions of the aesthetic tried to shield their world of cultural studies from the baser exchanges of the market. As a result, commerce and culture, economic thought and letters, were apportioned into their two separate domains, where for the most part, they remain (Crispin never meets the chairman of the Sun Corporation). He adds that "as a consequence, the juncture of these two aspects of life vanished from view, and the deep and unacceptable division *within* market culture reemerged as the deep but eminently acceptable division *between* the market and culture."[9]

9. Jean-Christophe Agnew, *Worlds Apart: The Market and the Theater in Anglo-American Thought, 1550–1750* (Cambridge: Cambridge University Press, 1986). See also Chapter 1 of Peter Stallybrass and Allon White, *The Politics and Poetics of Transgression* (Ithaca: Cornell University Press, 1986).

There is a fundamental questioning now and a refiguration of thought of the once taken-for-granted, largely obscured culture of capitalism, that is, of the larger, inclusive world of market culture. Agnew has addressed the formerly hidden issue of market and the rise of theater notably in England from 1550 to 1750. These are the very dates that enclose the early consolidation of the corporation, the singular social form, that made possible the institutional bases of colonization and trade in the British empire, the industrial revolution, and the contemporary national state.

In his study of the Dutch culture in its Golden Age, another cultural historian explicitly rejects the inclusion of the market, notably the role of the Dutch East India Company (VOC), but justified by appealing to our desire to comprehend the vernacular culture of the time, and he evokes richly textured pictures of the overwhelming wealth that collective enterprise through trade to the East had wrought.[10] Unfortunately what is missing is the legal-institutional trading framework intimately joined to the everyday culture of that affluent Dutch society.

Cultural historians since the successes of interdisciplinary history, achieved by members of the Annales school, have compelled us to confront the problematic that a millenium and especially the last four centuries of commercial development pose to the understanding. Simultaneous with the historians' attention to vernacular cultures and commerce, the social theorists respond to the same forces informed by political philosophy, and turn to solemn questions of human liberty as a problem of the growth of corporate power, whether that corporation be governmental or strictly private. "Why does it often appear that corporate actors such as large business corporations or large scale trade unions have gained excessive rights, while natural persons are helpless in their interactions with these corporate actors?"[11] The exquisite poignancy of this question remains unanswered, and it would appear that the scale of corporate power will continue to increase, forcing us with growing urgency to confront the challenge to our only recently acquired way of life.

In this general fascination with the problematics of culture, here briefly sketched, there are strange convergences occurring, such as those between the academy and the artworld. Artists as well as scholars plunge into the central maelstrom of our time and the result is a family resemblance between certain artists' work and those of academics. Two political artists, among many others, offer examples: Lothar Baumgarten and Hans Haacke.

Baumgarten, who lives as aesthetic ethnographer with native peoples

10. Simon Schama, *The Embarrassment of Riches: An Interpretation of Dutch Culture in the Golden Age* (New York: Knopf, 1987).
11. James S. Coleman, *The Asymmetric Society* (Syracuse: Syracuse University Press, 1982), p.54.

up to two years before a series of shows, juxtaposes in his installations the sign systems and names given by the European cultures to the cultural elements of non-Western peoples who have been invaded, placed on reservations, used as labor, murdered, sometimes studied and alternately ignored by the West. In the effort to clarify his position Baumgarten reflects:

> Though trapped in my Western thought patterns, I have always been interested in the "other"—the societies without a state—and in historical and social cohesion, the great anthropological nexus, the unconscious, which maintains a common thought process in mankind of which it is barely aware, and determines their actions by means of the dialogue of myths. I am making an analytical effort to free the historically and socially based reality from the imposed myths cloaking it, and to raise it by rational criticism to a metaphorical level, to art.[12]

Baumgarten pictures culture appropriating culture while Hans Haacke, in a series of controversial shows presented as overtly political acts, has taken on the critique of the culture of contemporary corporations as manifest in their writings and imagery.[13] He is particularly concerned with the way corporate players such as Mobil Corporation deploy imagery to further their economic interests in such places as South Africa despite compelling humanitarian reasons to act otherwise.

Haacke, through his own original research into the relevant documents, loves to draw out connections between powerful individuals, large firms (whether museum or oil company), and the making of images. The results of his investigations often comprise his shows. An art critic describes:

> *MetroMobiltan* (1985), is a compact construction requiring some scanning of type, but still intelligible at a glance, like an altarpiece. It deals with the partnership of two major American institutions: The Metropolitan Museum of Art in New York and Mobil Corporation, whose South African subsidiary, we learn, supplies the police and military of its host country with about twenty percent of their fuel needs.[14]

12. Lothar Baumgarten, "A Project for Artforum," *Artforum* (March 1988), p.108. See the announcement of Baumgarten's Paris show in *Artforum* (March 1987), pp.142–43.

13. Hans Haacke, *Hans Haacke: Unfinished Business*, Brian Wallis, ed. (Cambridge: MIT Press, 1986). See also, Jean Fisher, "Hans Haacke's Corporate Muse," *Artforum* (March 1987), pp.108–09.

14. Leo Steinberg, "Some of Hans Haacke's Works Considered as Fine Art," in *Hans Haacke*, p.17.

We see a convergence, then, in scholarship and in art between Culture (with a capital C although now High Culture has certainly fused in the East Village with Low Culture) and the economic marketplace. What I envisage takes from these and other sources: it is an ethnographic practice that aggressively uses a principled montage of methods and sensibilities that alternately describe, criticize, parody, and celebrate the world we have made. It can embrace a poetics of inquiry and comprehension as in the borrowing of the poets Williams and Stevens. The aesthetic and the scientific can be joined together in their antipathic strangeness as a source of energy for the task before us—to make sense of this world now: a world of a single, if differentiated, international market characterized by accelerating changes whose major forms of organization are large and small corporate structures and nation states—and of a single human species bound together by swiftly moving market exchanges of communications, persons and labor, capital, commodities and services. Regional and local cultural expressions affect and are affected by the international pricing system in which most phenomena, whether material or symbolic can be given a monetary value.

THE NEW ATLANTIS

Rather than overly relying on Marx's nineteenth-century belief that a class of capitalists motivated by avarice and through acquisitive interests exploits an urban proletariat, we discover an international system of corporations that, whether in concert or competiton, stimulates scientific activity for the purpose of turning their theoretically informed advances into consumer products for the market. In this realization, we add Francis Bacon of *The New Atlantis* to the Marx of *The Communist Manifesto,* and here I continue the sketch of a larger, mostly hidden, world in which ethnographers and the people of a specific locale such as South Philadelphia, Hazleton, or Chadds Ford inhabit but a minute niche.

"We sailed from Peru . . . " Bacon's fable, published in 1624, began.[15] A hundred and fifty men provisioned for a year set sail from the coast of South America for China and Japan. Blown off course, with no food, and having given up hope, they spotted land, "flat to our sight, and full of boscage; which made it shew the more dark." They made for it and found themselves in, as it was written, a good haven with a fair city behind it, on the island of Bensalem.

The existence of the islanders was unknown to the other countries of the Earth. Its cultural life was based entirely on a kind of international sci-

15. Francis Bacon, "The New Atlantis: A Work Unfinished." *The Complete Essays of Francis Bacon* (New York: Washington Square Press, 1963).

entific intelligence gathering. Members of a learned Foundation or College, an incorporated branch of the government, searched the kingdoms of Earth for practical—technological—information.

When the knowledgable returned from their stays with their collections of books, instruments, and patterns, they convened in the Order or Society of Salomon's House, also called the College of Six Days Works, the predatory institution that was at the heart of Bensalem society, the source of its scientific culture, its need for secrecy, and its sophisticated knowledge of nature.

It turned out that the distressed mariners were treated well on Bensalem because they proved themselves to be good Christians. After their quarantine, one of the executives of the College visited the city having been absent for twelve years while engaged in his studies. He allowed a special private meeting with one of the stranded men. The narrator of the account was chosen for the exclusive audience and the Father imparted to him a working knowledge of the state of Salomon's House. "First I will set forth unto you the end of our foundation. Secondly, the preparations and instruments we have for our works. Thirdly, the several employments and functions whereto our fellows are assigned. And fourthly, the ordinances and rites which we observe.

"The End of our Foundation is the knowledge of Causes, and secret motions of things; and the enlarging of the bounds of Human Empire, to the effecting of all things possible."

The Father then narrated a kind of encyclopedia of experimental sites and processes that acted on physical nature, animals and humans:

> We have dispensatories, or shops of medicines . . .
> We have also divers mechanical arts . . .
> We have also furnaces of great diversities . . .
> We have also perspective-houses, where we make demonstrations of all lights and radiations . . .
> We have also sound-houses, where we practise and demonstrate all sounds, and their generation . . .
> We have also engine-houses, where are prepared engines and instruments for all sorts of motions . . .
> We have also a mathematical house . . .

The men they sent to foreign countries were fellows of the College of Six Days Works and were referred to as the Merchants of Light. Then there were three fellows who on the return surveyed the literature, three who collected experiments in mechanical arts, three who conducted their own new experiments, three who compiled the experiments into tables so as to draw out axioms, and three who made from the others' work useful and practical things. Three groups of three men each followed those mentioned, and the last, called Interpreters of Nature, "raised the former discoveries by experiments into greater observations, axioms, and aphorisms." For those who made significant contributions, the tangible rewards included a statue of oneself in a gallery of one's scientific peers, and a space in an adjacent gallery to display one's inventions. The results of the work were published as a contribution to the branches of knowledge.

The scientific and technical sites were scattered in the area surrounding the city and indeed created a countryside of dispersed experimental locations.

> We have large and deep caves . . .
> We have high towers . . .
> We have great lakes both salt and fresh . . .
> We have also a number of artificial wells and fountains . . .
> We have also great and spacious houses . . .
> We have also fair and large baths . . .
> We have also large and various orchards and gardens . . .
> We have also means to make divers plants rise by mixtures of earths without seeds . . .
> We also have parks and inclosures of all sorts of beasts and birds . . .

It was a kind of great national foundation for experimentation with naturally occurring processes, that apparently took up and encompassed the entire nonurban landscape. There is in Bacon's vision, if we think of it at a general level, a kind of mapping to the contemporary siting of decentralized corporations in the U.S. (though we could easily include the world). Auto assembly lines, for example, are not restricted to Detroit but are placed in various states from California to New Jersey. Pharmaceutical firms have manufacturing facilities located in most of the larger cities of the country. Technologically sophisticated industry, then, as envisioned by Bacon and realized in this century, creates a particular landscape. Indeed, the entire world has become reinscribed during the nineteenth and twentieth centuries in both public and private sectors by corporations that manage science and technology for the making of products for consumption.

Bacon ended his treatise prematurely ["The Rest Was Not Perfected"] and it closed with the narrator bending down before the Father after his revelation of the sacred scientific center of the society to receive permission to publish the account of Bensalem's obvious successes with the experimental method.

In the final two sentences, Bacon has the Father gratuitously granting about two thousand ducats to the ship's members.

Although Bacon's written works have proved controversial and influential on scientific thought for three hundred years, his utopian Christian and scientific-technological polity has profoundly affected thought on national science policy in the competition between sovereign states. It became increasingly obvious that scientific and technological advantage, if not exaggerated Christian piety, were the central ingredients in economic competition.

For the uncompleted portion of *The New Atlantis* Bacon had proposed a frame of laws and commonwealth that would serve to advance the science and technology. He abandoned the proposal, thinking it would make the work too long. He did perceive, it appears, that the new scientific-technological order required a new political economy as well, but could not, I think, draft it.

To make the point that he was not well-equipped to write a utopian Commonwealth, consider that in his essay, "Of Plantations," he proposed that the best form of governance was a single strong man advised by counsel, preferably of gentlemen and not merchants. He was far off the mark. For by 1624 when the *Essays* were published, the Virginia colony had already elected its first representative assembly five years prior. The men elected to the annual assembly in the colony were no peasants, but were by today's standards small capitalist farmers and skilled craftsmen-traders and certainly not English aristocracy.

Note that the Bensalem island kingdom was not a market-driven economy. At best it was a poorly worked out system of corporations or government. The vaguely identified Foundation operated by international theft of what we presently legally define as intellectual property, as well as by experimentation, distribution, and despotic royal reward. We must join the Baconian vision to the international marketplace of commodities and ideas, the marketplace that dominates through the corporately organized institutions of the U.S. our everyday lives.

Our world does resemble that envisioned by Bacon more than three centuries ago, but with the addition of a global economy driven in part by a science and technology housed in large corporate structures.

* * *

My purpose in remarking on cultural and comparative studies with a digressive detour through Bacon's seventeenth-century visionary fable of a scientific-technological future as well as on the political art of Baumgarten and Haacke—and the earlier tour through the poetic landscapes of Stevens and Williams—is to emphasize the collisions and fusions (and the creative possibilities thus implied) between the arts and sciences and the academy and the art world in the larger, presently experienced economic context. This fusion results from the challenge to comprehend and simultaneously resist the culture of contemporary capitalism. It is an hegemonic condition that inundates us with its sheer abundance of corporately hidden processes and production of blinding surfaces of persuasive messages about how to use newly manufactured material things. An ethnography at once scientific and poetic contributes its modest and human-scale voice and imagery to those others engaged in such efforts to know and affect.

The entrepreneurs of CAN DO and the Brandywine River Museum and Conservancy engage in a complex and necessary mission of recolonization; for CAN DO, it is the refiguration of an extensive, old coalfield community; for the cultural toilers of the Brandywine, it is the remaking of upstream agricultural lands that once were farmed into the imagery of horse country and estates of the rich and whose legally controlled processes protect the upstream watershed for downstream consumption. In the devastated anthracite region and the picturesque piedmont of Andrew Wyeth we see two very different strategies for achieving institutional ends. For Boycie and the lower class black culture of the streets—however far that extends through the cities and countryside of America (and no one knows)—there is a precapitalist economy of face-to-face relations evolved if for no other effect than to secure the necessities and necessary pleasures from a social bottomland of the relative scarcities of capital and material.

Whether forged in the New World from African economic practices, or sui generis, I cannot say for certain, but the *hustle*, like black dialect, is doubly problematic. To those who would celebrate its practice as a distinctive cultural feature of black life, to obliterate *hustling* would amount to a form of genocide.[16] To political theorists, for whom such culturally specific considerations seem remote, the economy of the streets is a sore reminder that economic opportunity, as capitalist practice or marketplace competence, has imperfectly penetrated to the bottom of society. These two points of view represent the horns of a dilemma and contribute to the continuing and learnedly worried anxieties about American identities, cultural membership, and the civil effectiveness of the national body politic.

In the term used here, colonization, it would appear that black Ameri-

16. Some black intellectuals wish to subvert the hegemony of Euro-American discourse, the canon, by writing critique in dialect. Such a reversal offers significant possibilities for opening conversations toward a radical democracy of competing cultural sensibilities. I am assuming that the *hustle* offers an implicit critique—or the possibility of a critique—of capitalist exchanges, though I am not exploring that possibility here. On the cultural reversal of discursive practices see Henry Louis Gates, Jr., ed., *"Race," Writing, and Difference* (Chicago: University of Chicago Press, 1986), especially the opening remarks by Gates and the closing comments by Gates and Houston A. Baker, Jr.

can everyday life has been imperfectly gathered in and transformed by the culture of the market. In the 1980s the theater of the street, partially sealed off by exclusion and poverty, remained a vital, creative response that at once embraced and resisted the effects of colonizing—as the hard-edged vigor of rap music amply testified—of urban American conditions.

> Come on. My people,
> Can't you see
> Uh what's really goin' on?
> Unemployment's high,
> And the housin's bad,
> And the school's are teachin' wrong.
> Cancer from the water,
> Pollution in the air,
> But yer partyin' hard
> Like you jus' don' care
> Wake up ya'll
> You know that ain right
> Cause that hurts everybody
> Black or white.[17]

17. Brother D and Silver Fox, "How We Gonna Make the Black Nation Rise?" *Up Against the Beast* (MX Music, Reachout International Records A 130, 1984). For the complex relationships that developed between rap, domestic presidential politics, the American music business, and international racial politics, all within the black aesthetic critique of culture, see Danny Schechter, "Stetsasonic Rap," *Zeta Magazine* (February 1988), pp.46–47.

Journal Entry

29 May 1985

On the way to Mississippi to see my dying mother: cancer has spread from her colon to her liver to her lungs.

Why am I going? Is this my last time to see her? My sister has already arrived.

What am I doing—and my father?

What is he going to do?

I sit for a cup of coffee at an ARA Company vending unit in the airport.

The abstraction of airports.

The simplified landscape.

The post-coital calmness. Voices garbled over the ceiling loudspeakers.

I'm in trouble: Three pilots have ordered coffee from this terrible place.

My daughters.

My wife.

What does it all mean?

Where's all the feeling between mother and favored son?

Dissipated by time, any reality of it only a memory?

Would I write a bitter and remote elegy?

Her face blurred slightly as in a black and white photograph of her own Victorian cousins and aunts and uncles standing stiffly, unsmilingly in front of their prairie balloonframe house, no trees as far as the eye can see; a patchy yard of unmown grass. Seven faces. Blurred faces.

She had few memories to pass on. She wanted to live away from her children—five hundred miles away—a day's trip measured by driving the car.

In theory, each generation was to begin again, from scratch, brand new, no baggage, like the country.

In the dead of winter in 1983, ten days after winter solstice, I began a sabbatical leave from the university. My family and I flew to Bergen, Norway, where we rented a house in the northern suburb of Ulsetskogen. I offered a seminar in ethnographic field methods at the Sosialantropolgisk Institutt of the Universitetet i Bergen where I was a visiting professor of social anthropology. The daylight hours lasted only from ten in the morning until three in the afternoon. The rains began to seem interminable and it felt like spring would never come. My oldest daughter, just turning four, was unable to attend a daycare center because they were all fully enrolled, so she played on a supervised playground with other four-year-olds in the skin-eroding rain. Her cheeks and the backs of her hands became red and chapped raw. By May the days had grown imperceptibly longer, it seemed, and we knew it because the street lights winked out earlier in the morning, but the green and flowery signs of spring still appeared to develop so slowly as to be almost out of awareness and consigned to some indefinite future.

I had been corresponding with a former student in Sweden where I had lectured. He invited me to bring the family at the end of the spring term to spend the summer. He said he could find us a summer rental house on a beach in southern Sweden. After the dark wintery rains of Bergen, the beach with its images of hot sun and sand sounded like a welcome of light, warmth and dryness.

While my wife had traveled to Paris to meet her mother, I moved by train my two daughters and such household goods as we had with us from Bergen, Norway, to Lund, Sweden, where Bo greeted us, to no surprise, in yet another rain. After two days in Lund at Bo's apartment, he drove us to Angelsbacksstrand to our summer rental in a compound with another house. We unpacked our clothes and settled in to wait for Martha and her mother. I bought a blue Volvo station wagon from another academic to carry us all around during our summer sightseeing trips.

The lingering light of summer was a welcome relief from Bergen's damp darkness. My daughters spent their days at the beach. Next to our house, young girls pastured their horses. Looking in the opposite direction from the shore, we could see a silo break the skyline of the yellow, upward sloping wheat fields. Because I spoke neither Norwegian or Swedish, though everyone above the age of ten seemed to know English, I was suffering from some sort of sensory or cognitive deprivation. I became acutely aware of my surroundings, of the fields, of the mounds that prehistoric peoples had sculpted into place, of the slabs of stone, without writing, erected long ago presumably by those same little-known prehistoric people, but still standing in the countryside.

At night when I lay down I could hear water gurgling beneath the house, as if a stream were whispering through some underground channels.

When I asked, people said that perhaps what I heard was the reservoirs beneath the houses filling with fresh water. Or perhaps it was the sewers. I was told that the whole of southern Sweden was sewered, farms as well as denser settlements. Where the children played on the beach there was a dark oozing that on some days smelled badly. Walking to the beach one morning, we saw that a door set in a mound on the sand was open and there was a building beneath. It was a buried sewage treatment plant that ejected its waste in the packed sand beneath the Atlantic shoreline where our children played.

I began yet another draft of a book on my field research among black Americans. I worked in a bedroom connected by an outdoor walkway to our main house. The privacy and seclusion were useful, though I was suffering from too much semantic seclusion already. One morning I drove my Volvo with my notes and blank paper and parked at the end of a road that faced a boulder-strewn strand overlooking the Atlantic. I was working on my writing when suddenly I heard a sound that seemed to originate far below the ground. It was as if two mountains had suddenly collided underground with a single deafening impact. It was the sound of gigantic rock on rock. I looked around, but there was no tremor or shaking and the noise did not repeat itself. I couldn't figure out what it was or why it seemed terribly gigantic and yet from deep in the ground. I asked people about it and no one could do anything but speculate. There was no answer.

Not more than fifteen kilometers from where we lived was an airfield that was at once a civilian airport and a national defense airfield. During the fine weather on the beach with vacationers from Stockholm down for two months at their summer homes, the heavy SAAB jets stayed on the ground at the airfield. Come August fourteenth with the end of the season, the jets climbed into the air and screamed up and then down the beach in tight formation day after day. I thought that if a country wanted to invade Sweden it would be best to do it during the height of the summer beach season. One afternoon driving with my wife and daughters by the airfield, itself carved from the large agricultural estates that once dominated the southern Swedish landscape, I looked at the disguised hangars for the jets, and noticed that what appeared to be snorkels and other air exchanging openings ruptured the ground at several places.

As a result of this observation and my earlier experience, I asked one of our Swedish acquaintances who was highly placed in a pan-Nordic governmental position if there were military installations beneath the ground in our part of Sweden. I described what I had heard and seen and she told me she would look into it. Later she said that on good information she had learned that there were no underground installations in that part of the country. I believed her and had no reason to question her veracity. My curiosity was more or less laid to rest. A few days later, I was sitting on the grass playing with the girls in a small city not far from Angelsbacksstrand while my wife shopped. I looked at the vegetation, and much to my surprise, saw a series of pipes that poked out of the ground. They resembled what I had seen near the airport. Added to them was a modest aerial of the sort for receiving radio signals. When Martha joined us and we ate lunch on the lawn I showed her what I had seen. I wanted a reality check to prove I was not over-imagining or hallucinating.

With the sensory deprivation from the winter weather in Bergen, the semantic deprivation of foreign countries which included a thirteen day trip through Western Europe I made alone on which I had exactly two conversations of any duration, and with the strange underground Sweden that I experienced but could not at first imagine, and with my fieldnotes of the study of black life in South Philadelphia, and with my distance and yet preoccupation with America from that oceanic separation, I turned toward a poetic kind of fiction, a fictional ethnography to express myself and to make some sort of document of the whole crazy mix I felt and that I confronted starkly day-to-day. Even the contrasts seemed exaggerated: a squeaky-clean, crime-free Sweden and a filthy, dangerous Philadelphia.

I induced in myself an oneric flight through America. My imaginings were not of blacks per se, nor of whites, nor really of anything specific. A kind of free-floating imagery spilled out and I wrote it down in that bedroom next to the summer house. I did not write the ethnography that I wanted to work on but drafted a piece of fictional poetics of life in America as a total stranger to it might find it—a young ethnographer—not the America of reality, but the America as a fictional construct. Through the imaginative revery, it became a country that was not so much a *place* as a bizarre culture generated through the application of theoretical scientific principles.

6
The Masks

Female Fig Leaf. 1961 bronze cast of 1950 plaster, 3½ × 5¾ × 5″. Philadelphia Museum of Art, given by Mme. Marcel Duchamp. Reproduced by permission.

From a Letter to His Mother

I was dropped off at the edge of the city and felt the surge of lone-liness and isolation I feared. As I looked for transportation my feelings were soon interrupted by the eerie feeling that something terrible had happened and as a result everything in the city had come to a halt. By our own standards it was a weekend, so I expected it would be dif-ficult to find ways of getting about, but I also saw no people walking around. . . .

As usual my curiosity got the best of me and I knocked on several doors. No answers. I decided to go down the block, which was terraced from house to house and was quite steep, and kept knocking on doors. Finally I just went in to the fifth house when there was no answer there either. They are very differently arranged than ours—but I'll go into that later. In what was a child's or adolescent's room, I was totally shocked to find the remains of someone on the floor. All sorts of thoughts and anxieties flooded through me. I tried to stifle a fugitive surge of anger that someone I came to study was not alive!

I can't tell you in words the beginning of the near-paralysis that spread through me. I had come to study living people and I experienced a growing suspicion that everyone there was dead. I went from house to house in horror and almost hatred, touched with pity and a terrible sense of loss for the people who were no longer alive, for the sheer waste of their humanness, for the daily lives cut off, mother from child, just like that. I think maybe everyone is dead. . . .

What gets me is that they are all dead and I am trapped. I cannot leave this place now. Everything has changed for me. I came to talk to people and they will never speak again. A whole way of life van-ished—the cultural loss. I came to dance and drink, and learn their way of doing almost anything, and now nothing. I have to turn myself into an archaeologist. If I had wanted to be an archaeologist and exhume graveyards I would have taken up with Dr. Barraes and his students. They were a bright bunch, but that is not the point. I did learn a few things from them, maybe I'll have to put that to good use now. Sorry, I didn't mean to sound self-pitying. . . .

From a Letter to His Advisor

When I first found all the bodies I did not immediately note that each person had worn a mask. On closer inspection, now, I find that without exception each person, even the tiniest babies, were apparently masked. At least I think they were. There is associated with each head, a mask covering the face, or head, or in such close proximity that it could only have been worn when the person was alive. The masks must have changed positions a bit as the body decayed. I am finding masks everywhere and think this may be in some way central to the cultural values of these people. The masks sure dominated everyday life as far as I can tell. . . .

I don't mean to sound nonprofessional, but I am so damn lonely, and all this death around me, signs of it everywhere, deserted vehicles with masked remains; houses, shopping areas, workers' areas, administrative quarters, everything. . . .

I am suffering from necrophobia, certainly not necrophilia. So far I have not touched one of those masks. I've photographed quite a few, and done some drawings of them. . . .

From a Letter to a Friend

I have not put my fingers on any of the numerous masks I've found, but I am going to one of these days.

The masks, by the way, are found in all sizes. They all seem to cover the face, and there the uniformity ends. It's hard to generalize at this point. Sometimes the whole head is covered as if the mask were extended to a helmet. At other times the mask covers the head and face, shoulders, and upper torso, leaving the arms free. Since there are human skeletons inside, I am not going to move them around. Not yet. Somewhere in the back of my mind I believe these people are not dead, or others are alive and will come to the city one day in great caravans bearing the mournful living to bury their loved ones.

Still and all, I'm going to try on some of these masks one of these days. At least I'll get to participate in the culture after all. Once I have the mask on, I'll pretend to be one of the people of the city in the persona they wore. . . .

Maybe if I wore just one mask I could move around the city and begin to reconstruct who, where, and why. For some reason I am not fascinated with the cause of their deaths, but with the course of their lives. It would help if I could decipher the written language. I had expected to learn it from people I spoke with every day.

From a Fieldnote Entry

2 October. Today I may have discovered a site where masks were manufactured. It was a large complex in one of the districts near the center of town. I have not finished mapping the complex, but the major outlines seem to be something like this (from a quick walk through).

Ritual masks Religious?	Scientific masks
Sports masks	Administration, Research, Library, and Receiving
Everyday and Occupational masks	Unclassified area (yet to do)

I have been unable to classify fully the occupational masks, but expect to begin again tomorrow. If I find one completed I'll wear it—[personal note].

From a Letter to His Mother

I'm sorry I sounded so depressed in my last few letters but I really *was* down. Death and not life. What a shock, what tragedies multiplied a hundred thousand times. . . .

What's new is that I may be pulling out of it. That should make you happier with my situation. I know how you hate for me to be and to say I am depressed. Since I found some sort of manufacturing center for the masks, at least some of them, I have decided to try one on and sort of go exploring inside the thing. I've been here more than a month now, I think I have to go for it. If I can find a completed face mask tomorrow I'll try one on. I've been mapping the factory I found today and am very tired. Tonight I am going to fall asleep deciding if I'll try on a sports mask or an occupational mask. I feel I need to know more, much more. . . .

From a [Partial] List of Observed [But Uncategorized] Masks

1. Masks with frescoes
2. Masks and bandages
3. Masks resembling radios, typewriters, shoes, pipes, coffee cups, shoats, urns, buses, ice cubes
4. Masks of birds, domestic and wild cats and dogs, fish, elephants, giraffes, a bar of soap, the sky at night, pancakes, raccoons
5. Flotation masks
6. Eating masks
7. Reading masks
8. Biologically active masks

From a Fieldnote Entry

16 October. My idea was to do a thorough investigation of the factory administrative section and find the director's office. I thought there might be something there. There was. It was the only fully assembled, uninhabited mask I have found and that is the one I am going to try on. I am going to proceed like this: first I'll log all my movements and record impressions; then I'll try on the mask and keep a running tape-recorded account of the experiences; then with it on, I'll go exploring. I figure that if I have on the mask of the executive officer, I'll have on some sort of official and powerful thing.

0.0 See 15 October notes for description of executive office.

0.1 The uninhabited mask is hanging in a small closet-like room but is connected to sockets in the walls by three connectors. These may lead to a kind of power supply or this tiny room may be a recharging unit.

0.2 I carefully unplug the hanging mask from the sockets and nothing happens. No change in sound, etc., when I do so. Perhaps the mask is no longer powered, in a way dead, like the people.

0.3 The mask itself hangs suspended from the ceiling with a strong cable attached to the top of the helmet. This is quite a full mask, and it rests on the shoulders, covers the back and chest, and leaves openings for the arms and torso. Getting in could be a job.

0.6 I am inside the mask and while the original owner and I are a bit different in proportions, I can stand inside it without too much difficulty. The interior is soft. I cannot tell if it is heavy or not. Next step: disconnect ceiling cable and bear the full weight. I will explore the factory first with this mask on since I think it is the situationally appropriate thing to do.

1.0 With the mask on I can see and hear okay and it is not particularly heavy but the mask is not docile. I hear no sounds emanate from the mask, but I don't feel quite like myself, that is, I do not feel the way I usually feel about myself—[pursue this in following fieldnotes].

2.0 I am in the section I titled "Everyday and Occupational Masks" and am apparently in the public sector, i.e., civil service. There are tables, lockers for hanging masks, and so on; it is not an assembly line, but rather organized as a series of work stations. As I enter this area, the workers do not turn around, or look toward me in any way that I can visually discern from inside my mask. For some reason I have the idea that their masks register my presence and communicate it to them. All the workers are busy but at a deliberate pace. I feel a bit strange and am having a reexperience of this very city. I must record it, though standing here while I do so does not feel quite proper.

2.1 I am beginning to reimagine this city, which I am discovering is composed of two conceptual points. I do not at this time wonder how I can both be here and reimagine the city simultaneously.

It is an extensive, if flat, urban space. In the very center of the city is one point, the central place. All other points of the city stretching in every direction are identical to each other, hence are the same point. This is the entire two pointed city.

We can have equal access to both points. We can go anywhere. The entire city is undifferentiated. Everything is painted white or made of white marble. If we imagine a single difference, say, the philosopher's patch of blue, this will no longer be the same city. We will lose our way. We will wander around aimlessly. There will be no place to buy lunch.

patch
of
blue

4.0 I must stop my record of observations to say that the mask, while I have been wearing it, has *increased the volume*. I do not know any other way of putting it. Inside this thing I experience the world with a more dreamlike quality. I want to be precise about that statement. I feel that I am one-half in charge of my flow of experiences and I feel that the mask, like a dream, or unconscious stream, is one-half in charge of my experiences. It is as if I can only partially shape what I feel and the mask partially shapes what I feel. Something like that at least.

5.1 The sports section. One of the workers, wearing what appears to be a brief, protective mask, is assembling something. When I draw closer to look over his shoulder I have a sudden encompassing experience, a kind of surge of knowledge about what he is doing. It is odd since we have not verbally communicated. Perhaps this work station and the activities are coded with signals that activate the rig I am wearing. I will try to document what I experienced as I watched the worker put together mask number 307.

Four small suction cups are affixed to the forehead and from each suction cup there is a small hook attached.

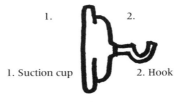

1.   2.

1. Suction cup   2. Hook

From the hook a light chain mail curtain covers the face to the neck. There are no drawstrings attached that would open the curtain to reveal the full face.

Custom-made perforations, outlined in metal like grommets, are needed so that the sight-lines may be established through the flexible metal screen.

While horseback riding, it is advisable to fasten the bottom of the curtain so that it does not whip about the face, causing lacerations. Something like string may be looped through the lower corners of the covering and fastened with hooks embedded in leather straps around the shoulders or on the chest.

7.0 I am walking through the occupational section on my way out. I need to fill out my notes and key them to the voice-activated comments. I think I am tired, I can't really tell inside this thing. This is my last subsection until tomorrow.

7.2 Traveling masks all around me. These people are obviously highly mobile. I stop at a section with four people and rather complex robotic machinery. My mind wanders and I cannot concentrate on the production processes. I feel that I am a traveler, yet I have traveled very little here, confining myself to the city. I'll voice-record what I sense, then I'll analyze it later; I need all the raw data I can get.

7.3 Most of all it resembles blocks of wood connected in a row by hooks and eyes, looking much like a train. Each block of wood is set on dowels which keep them rolling on track as the whole string of cars moves into a predetermined future.

For potential passengers, two problems seem almost insurmountable. The first is how to obtain a ticket that is properly worded in order to ride to a precise destination in their own uncertain futures; the second is how to conceptually board an object that resembles nothing so much as an interconnected string of wooden blocks set on dowels.

To obtain the ticket, with its syntax, complex tense system, and tiny writing on the back that employs the proper terms, the potential passengers use the ultra-computer counter near the central waiting room. The difficulties are both very straightforward and completely baffling. The behavioral core of the ultra-computer totally realigns *all* future schedules when a single user punches in a temporally sophisticated request.

Boarding the train proves a different challenge, no less demanding. Point A has to be connected to point B in the mind of the passengers before the conductor admits them. The time lines, like the spokes of a bicycle wheel are splayed in all directions simultaneously. At the cry of the conductor or the shrill whistle of the switchman, the blocks, which look like wood, lurch forward, sometimes tossing the commuters backward or forward in time, depending on which way they are facing.

From a Letter to His Mother

Last night, after wearing the executive mask all day, I fell asleep with it on and woke up this morning. Despite its fullness, it was not uncomfortable. While I feel a little bit strange, even as I write this to you, I am comfortable with the experience. I heard a music last evening but I cannot tell where it came from and I was too tired to investigate.

It went like this:

————————————————————————————————→

bu po bu po bu po bu po

     uho   uho   uho   uho   uho   uho

        bumn   bumn   bumn   bumn   bumn

ah ah ah ah ah ah ah ah ah ah ah ah ah ah ah ah

and I could only believe that the sounds made by voice and machine (instrument) were one. . . .

From a Fieldnote Entry

17 October. I am on my way to the factory. It might as well be called the ritual design center of this society, I believe. Today I expect to wear my executive mask right into the sacred section—religion, art, ritual—whatever the fine classification proves to be.

Log from 17 October

10.0 Art section. I see an eye that appears on the outside ring to be white laced with miniature red veins. Then there is a deep brown, but smaller ring inside the white one. A black dot has been placed exactly in the middle of the brown. These concentric circles complete the eye. The eye itself is set in a square, brushed chrome plate; and the blinking of the fleshy eyelid contrasts in its lifelike movement with the chrome.

10.3 I am walking down the shop floor and stop to look at another piece.

The base is rather large and painted a highly reflective red enamel. Fastened to the base are three support vanes painted a flat black, no higher than the average human. On top of the vanes a platform is riveted that has the same red enamel color. Five blue spheres lie on the red platform. Where the blue globes touch the red platform, a light purple aureole appears. A single aerial juts upward from the topmost ball. It is a silver foil with a blunted tip. Even in moderate wind it whips slightly back and forth. Today, no signals leave or enter the aerial.

Log from 18 October

18.02 There are numerous ritual masks. In the architect's office, sketches proliferate and are tacked on the walls from floor to ceiling. Little maquets of newly designed facial coverings hang from the ceiling at different altitudes. There is a dazzling wealth of work done here. The ideas proliferate like mad. I am really at the sacred center of this masked society. Only I understand nothing.

18.04 I am examining a small device that I have seen implanted in other masks as they have been assembled. No use in trying to stop the flow of impressions [I cannot record fast enough—am losing some of it—but here goes anyway].

18.05 The man is entirely naked and has a normal size erection. Above the erect penis is the belly with the necessary scar of an appendectomy. Above the belly is the chestal area, the shoulders, arms, hands, fingers, and so on. On the neck and head is a mask (to be described elsewhere).

At the great annual parties marking the turning of the seasons, the honorable man, the man of strength, vigor, power, and pure animal magnetism, is he who stays aroused latest into the night. All the men are carefully watched (one assumes) for collective judgments to be made on he who is strongest, most virile, and who has, despite food, drink, physical activity, and fatigue, an erection at the end.

The ranking or public evaluations of others at these parties, such as women, is based on quite different criteria.

19.00 The interior [this section is missing]. . . .

Structural members: the outer skin demands strong but light internal trusses. Most of the support members were modeled on the early bridge-building experiments. Inside the artificial skin, the exceedingly light and thin alloy frameworks are built up. It is essential from the first planning stages that the entire structure be designed to bear not only the outer skin of whatever fabric, but that certain additions, which might cause stress, such as motors, doors, flaps, blinders, wind screens, turbines, cable anchorings, hallogen lamps, or pulleys, be theoretically considered.

Some of the structural members are so exceedingly light and thin that they are not much more than conceptual frameworks.

Outer skin: the outer skin, visible from the street, can be made of synthetic or natural fibers. Very few of these fibers are ever constructed from first principles.

The fabric skin, stretched over the frame has to be taut. Then the skin must eventually be lacquered, shellacked, enamelled, or epoxied in any color combination desired.

Positioning the slits for the eyes is an all-important step. Indeed, the best facial covering is always made to order for the individual. Designers have to consider in advance the optional openings for sound: sound production, speech and music, and monitoring the airwaves. Failure to provide voice projection openings (permanent, remote controlled, or manual) would render the human wearing the frame-and-fabric construction, speechless.

Presentation: mask architecture perhaps exacts the most excruciating toll on the person of all the arts. Long apprenticeship, infinite care, genius, and a profound and subtle sense of the sacred are ingredients of the mix. Worldly success may be denied the architect. The monument that is born, however, cannot be destroyed for it is etched into the local materiality of the universe. A mask cannot be unmade. Facing as it does the gods, themselves etched into the locality, the ceremony for presenting the new mask is undertaken with considerable risk and great care.

Once finished, the new mask is shrouded in grey, 100% polished cotton cloth. It is then carefully mounted blind on the wearer who is led to the podium. The applause begins. From random sources, music appropriate to the mask is played.

A speech is given, often by a professional orator. His fees are paid for either by the consortium or the artist whose words he uses.

After the semi-private ritual address to the audience, the mask is unveiled and a magnum of champagne is forcibly smashed against the mask, or, if the mask is delicate and intricate, against the podium. The person wearing the new mask is then launched into the crowd. If any one of the assembled people guesses the exact identity of the wearer, the wearer is disgraced and the artist given a probationary warning.

From the Initial Translation of Materials in the Library Collection of the Design Center

A. Records of unmasking from the dawn of humanity to the present.

B. The vocabulary of fixed facial expressions.

C. *Fable of the First Mask*

D. "The Role of Masks in the Recent and Far Future Evolution of the Isotropic Universe from a Fixed Vantage Point" (title of a scholarly article).

E.1 From the rule books (hundreds of volumes): "When masks are designed, fictitious heads, arms, genitals, feet, legs, or whatever can be designed into the overall structure. Use of any other equipment such as straps, carrying cases, pre-installed portable toilets, and lights . . . is encouraged by income tax deductions. Consult tables from RS (Revenue Service)."

E.2 "Full body masks signify danger and all citizens are to be warned when one wearing such a mask appears in the local visual environment."

E.3 "The *reality principle* shall not hold from this day forth. . . ."

From His Chronicle of the Early Days

I returned to the Director's office after three days of wearing his mask. As I entered the room I knew immediately he was there. I heard pleasant laughter as I walked through the door. He was laughing aloud and greeting me and speaking polite sentences in his language. This was the first person who spoke to me and I was extremely surprised and very relieved to see how open and warm his greeting was, as if he had been expecting me, as if in his mind, I had already arrived. Obviously since I had taken the liberty of visiting the design assembly floor of the factory someone must have provided clearance. He had to be the person who had arranged it without my knowing it.

There was too much I did not know.

Through gestures he invited me to his home and we were taken there by car. The building in which he lived was a residential one, about five or six stories tall and his quarters covered the whole top floor and part of the roof. On the roof was an immaculate formal garden, and along one side of the building was his art gallery with paintings and sculptures, free standing musical machines, and photographic images.

Using words, diagrams, and gestures, he introduced me to a woman named Laurea, his wife, I believed, and let me know they had five children. The children were nowhere around.

The three of us walked to the formal garden, right to the edge and looked down. I could see three couples below us talking to each other, standing, I thought, too close together.

No sound floated up to us from their voices. Perhaps the masks they wore were tuned to the same radio frequency and they were

ON THE AIR

to one another.

Laurea offered me a drink identical to the one she had made for herself and the Director made one for himself. As she handed me mine, I looked closely at the mask she was wearing. It covered her head completely and the front was occluded by an opaque veil of tan and pink. Since I could not see in, I assumed she could not see out. At the top of the head was an ocular scanning unit of somewhat unique design and I believe that she was wired into a viewing unit and could not see me directly. I wondered if there were any significance in indirect viewing. The Director's mask resembled the one I was wearing—quite bulky to look at, but not at all heavy to wear. I was certainly convinced as I sipped my drink in silence, watching the leaves of the box elders twitch quietly in a light wind, that I had no idea of the numerous functions of the mask I was wearing.

Interrupting our silence there on the roof overlooking the city, the Director drew an impromptu floor plan of the penthouse and invited me to live with them while I conducted my anthropological field studies of their society. I agreed to very readily and was shown a bit later to my room and adjoining toilet facilities. I was also given a set of new keys, the most intricate of which unlocked a row of lockers in my room where masks were to be kept. Each locker was empty and the implication was that I was to acquire my own set of masks, or so I thought at the time.

For the next few months I devoted myself to the mastery of the language. I assembled insofar as I could a complete list of phonemes, tried to get down all the morphemes, and labored over the syntax, tonality, speed, dialect differences (?), and all the rest. My linguistic studies were made all the more difficult by the masks everyone wore. Most masks altered sound so that often I could not tell what sounds were in the language and what effect on speech the masks made.

After four months of wandering the city, buying things so I could talk with the shopkeepers (and obtain the numerical and formulaic bartering system they used), visiting the factories, homes, and attending public events, I had mastered a rudimentary speaking ability and was learning new words and phrases each day.

The five children of the Director and Laurea were two females and three males. They were all living away from the family quarters because they had reached maturity. One of the daughters returned to visit her parents, bringing a man with her. She was about my age while he seemed a bit older. I was attracted to her, although I obviously could not see her face. Her mask was simple and tasteful as was her male companion's, and I thought the masks had been carefully designed to resemble one another. But not too much so.

What fascinated me in particular was that she wore a modified duchamp wedge of chastity which meant she could not comfortably sit down. I wondered about the meaning of this, but was afraid, for some reason, to ask. At mealtimes we all ate standing up.

The modified duchamp wedge of chastity, had fine silver wire from the front running out of her pubic hair, up her belly and across her navel, between her breasts, and the wire was fastened to a choker around her throat. At the back of the plug, a similar wire ran between her buttocks upward along her spine and was fastened to the back of the choker. I assumed that the wires kept the plug from falling out.

I could see her eyes, naked behind the mask, and they were a pale grey flecked with blue and green. I looked directly at her eyes, though I am unsure that she could see mine. The smoked glass covering of my mask was very dark and may have shaded my eyes completely. The attitude of my body and mask as I looked at her surely gave away my inquisitive gaze, I was convinced. She looked at me in an even, neutral way which challenged me, I suppose, to try to render her look less even and flat. In brief passing glances I examined her body which was nicely proportioned. Her brown nipples and their delicate aureole were stimulating to me. There was no way I could speak to her alone, for unfortunately there was no opportunity. I would like to have had sex with her and to have altered her poise, but the man she was with was constantly standing beside her and tediously talking. When I looked toward him I would watch her with my peripheral vision and thus gained an indirect, more fantasied impression of her than I would have had if she and I had been alone.

That night I lay awake thinking about her, recreating her in different situations, trying to bracket her friend, and removing, in my mind, her choker. Since I could not sleep I began to explore the mask I was wearing which seemed exceptionally complex, and one which, like the language, needed thorough and systematic study.

Although I cannot report exactly how it came about, as I lay in the darkness (or perhaps got up and walked) I began to monitor the relationship between the Director and Laurea who were in their own quarters, adjacent to mine. This is a bit of what went on there: Laurea pried off his left thumbnail as he slept. Beneath the thumbnail in a pink cavity of new skin was a toggle switch, a prosthetic device of bone, nerves, and flesh that she could move into four positions, like the four points of the compass. His face mask came away as she flicked the switch back. Her adjustment to the switch revealed not his face but the portion of bone and cartilege just in back of his face. Apparently mask and face were united in such a way that the face would not be uncovered when that particular mask flipped open.

Such a dramatic event narcotized him and she then moved the switch into another position. At that, his left leg split open beneath the knee along a seam on the shin bone. The front of the bone looked like a long, narrow door that ratcheted outward to reveal inside thin rods of smooth, whitish celluloid or high technology plastic. She removed the rods one at a time and with some joints she took from the drawer of the night table, she fastened the rods into a structure. The construction resembled a geodesic frame or a high school model of atomic nuclei.

In the morning, as they were standing on the roof with their daughter and her man, near the garden, holding cups, the Director was berating Laurea in a voice mediated by his mask. He rasped in low threatening tones,

"—when I dream. Don't mess with those. The dreaming goes awry when you do that. . . ."

And so on. I tried not to listen but my mask amplified their every word.

From the Personal Notebook: Lovers' Masks

I told her I would meet her that evening. She knew that I was not from the city, so she explained to me that I was to wear a lover's mask. Since I did not own one, I was forced to find one. I was a bit embarrassed to ask someone to help me find such a mask in the first place and then to wear such a mask in public—stating to everybody my intentions—in the second place. To make a long story short, I was able to find a lover's mask at the factory in the everyday life section and it was fitted to me personally that afternoon. The mask itself surprised me for it very nearly violated one of the central rules for the use of masks.

Lovers' masks cover most of the body and this is one of the main reasons that they cannot be bought off the rack. They have to be fitted for you. Since the full body mask taboo held everywhere, the lover's mask was exempt from that violation by the use of a window. In most of them the genitals were left open to visual inspection by a glass or plastic window. Some of the masks just had round porthole shaped windows with no glass in them at all. The one I chose had a glass window and was an expensive, top-of-the-line model. Also the mask came in sections that could be removed a piece at a time until it came to the last facial coverings which could only be removed by the person wearing it and not another. From the construction of the large covering I figured, rightly, that each lover removed pieces from the mask of the other, like moving through a preordained series of religious pilgrimages but with a relocated set of intentions.

After we met at the proper time and location, we drove to a safe house, enjoyed a delightful dinner, and settled in for the evening. After dinner she began to sing and she sang all the songs of the region where she grew up as a child. Then she shifted to songs about the universe and wrote out the words. We sang together and the musical machines accompanied us or we kept tune with them.

————the suns migrate around themselves in a snake dance
little fingers of gravity
holding little fingers of smoke
four billion years go by.

Then an
infinite X of universes, each soundless
fills with galaxies
photons never meet across this reach
they bounce into themselves
and wink asleep.

Out of darkness sheer light dazzles fireworks
from everywhere while turning weightless
in the night sky.

Along the time lines
universes flow off screen from the sacred
random center.

This will go on forever

She asked me if I recognized the librettos and I had to admit that I did not. She explained that the woman, Laurea, had written them, that she was the official poet of the city. It made me feel imminent just to be singing her stuff.

Making love was perhaps more demanding than I expected, and I will only summarize. Her mask, which promised to fit her body closely when at first I saw her, was an illusion sustained through most of our time together. When I began the languid removal of parts of the mask, say, over a thigh or breast, the part of the body that the outlines of the mask promised was not there. It was a mask of tactical illusions. Everything was just slightly off. As I attempted to open the window to the genital area I found that the glass port I removed was a painted or photographed copy of the area, not a window on the person at all. I do not know if this was a violation of the full body mask code or not.

From His Chronicle: The Bolinder-Munktell

There was no breakfast served in the house of the Director. I was used to a breakfast so I found ways to make do. In early spring the Director offered to let me use his car whenever I wished so I could get around the city more easily to conduct my fieldwork. I was indeed grateful. He never drove the car, he told me, and it just sat in the parking garage in the basement.

In the evening he gave me the keys. The next morning I got up and went down to the parking garage intent on driving the car to a coffee shop that served breakfast.

His car was a big Bolinder-Munktell in *concours* condition. I unlocked it and could tell that it had not been driven in a long time. I started it up and the deeply satisfying rumble of the engine stirred in my stomach. From the driver's chancel I noticed on the passenger side that there was a miniature planetary surface on the dashboard. I had seen these tiny garden-like artforms before, but this one had its own weather system—that was unbelievably rare. Some of the landscape was under cloud cover and it appeared that an infinitely tiny rainstorm was underway over one of the major land masses. I could barely discern with the unaided eye the fields, shorelines, deserts, stands of virgin forest, gardens, canals, settlements, roads, aqueducts, and inland lakes of the continents. I would have to come back and get photographs of this, I thought.

As I drove into the morning sunlight, I glanced at the dashboard again and I could see the cloud cover begin to dissipate from the surface and it was as if a greenness began to intensify in color, even as I turned the first corner.

I cannot say how happy I was to be behind the wheel of the Bolinder-Munktell.

As I turned into the coffee shop parking lot, I was just behind a new Funki-Boythorpe painted a midnight green. I parked beside it in the lot. A man got out with sleepy deliberation, as I did, and we more or less met on the walk in front of the cars. He spoke first and said that one did not see many Bolinder-Munktells any more. He was keying to my Director's mask as he spoke. Before I could answer him I had to digest the fact that he wore the most elaborate bio-active mask I had yet seen. There seemed to be many divisions to it, like the striations of muscle or certain sea creature colonies. I checked my amazement and responded that I also admired his Funki-Boythorpe. I added that I had never driven one and asked him how he liked driving it. He described briefly how the vehicle accelerated, shifted, and cornered compared with the Triumphs and Defeats he had previously owned.

We continued our conversation as we ambled into the coffee shop and sat near one another at the counter. We both made indirect comments about one another's masks so as to draw the other out conversationally. After we were served *zoega* and circular pastries with the middles blown out of them by brief explosions, I revealed to him that I was an anthropologist studying his society and was focusing at the present on the mask factory (formerly the Android Manufacturing and Repairing Company or AMARCO as it is now called). He seemed a bit reluctant to reveal the connection between himself, his mask, and his occupation, but finally it came out that he was employed at the AMARCO mask factory in the section I had never visited. His mask, it turned out, was an *Enhancer* which is the most elaborate mask in the society. The bio-active masks enhanced the entire processes of the human organism—thoughts, emotions, reaction times, and interpersonal contact—however one directed it. Most of the *Enhancer* masks, I learned, were worn by theoreticians and I was talking to one of the key section heads of the mask factory, theoretical division.

We introduced ourselves, finally. His name was John, and he invited me to the theoretical division and said he would enjoy cooperating with me fully on my anthropological studies.

He invited me to visit him that very day, and I felt I had made a definite breakthrough. I was hoping that he might become a key informant which we anthropologists cherish and rely upon so much. I felt keenly that I needed to know the central tenets of this social and cultural system. I was certain that if anyone could tell me what they were, it would be the theoreticians. I had to assume that they worked self-consciously at the presuppositions every day, on the job (I am aware, of course, of the counter-argument which is that they are *not* self-consciously working at an entirely explicit level).

Right after lunch John showed me around the floor of the theoretical division, then surprised me by saying that this was just the surface, and that there was an underground labyrinth that underlay the entire city, countryside, and the phenomenal world. In the labyrinth, the various sciences were located with their offices and laboratories. The maze of rooms was connected to the surface of the city and the theoreticians tended to live in enclaves near the vertical commuter lines that descended underground to their sections.

He explained to me that the mission of the theoretical section was simple. The theoreticians were working toward a synthesis—a grand synthesis—of the post-real universe. Such an integration, he told me, depended on a unification of physical elements, chemical reactions, and living organisms (including humans) as simulated, amplified, and modified by a masked polity. There is more to it than this, he said, but I felt I was really on to something.

More often than not, for the next several weeks, he and I met informally at breakfast, and we would talk, sometimes about theory, sometimes about the mystery of life.

Several months later, John and I were talking on the surface of the theory section. He told me that he thought we knew one another well enough so that he could give me the straight story. That caught me off guard for I felt in his tone that it might be something personal. He told me that before I arrived in the city I had been expected. That was a shock to me because I believed that I had entered the situation completely cold. He went on to add that people there had contrived to direct the course of my research: in brief, I had been set up. His revelation sent me into a rage inside although he could not see how I felt since my face was covered and the rest of my body would not register the emotions that my face could.

After this revelation he digressed to tell me how all humans secreted crisscrossing trails throughout their lives at once spatial and temporal. The trails were something like that left by ants. He told me how older people relived their lives by going over their old pathways (memory traces, etc.) and crossing the trails left by someone interesting they could get lost, never to return to their friends and family. He explained that the trails could also be normative. A path for someone could be set down in advance, like predestination or like the positivist's belief in scientific prediction. The advance pathways would force the person to certain areas, certain life chances, certain discoveries and revelations, and most certainly, away from particular secrets, persons, insights, or ideas. I grew more furious, for I saw that this applied to me. His account of the constraints under which I was now working made me determined that by using the scientific method I could break through and find the sacred center of society and use it, if not for revenge, then certainly to break from the role into which I had been cast.

There are two political parties, he told me, that are competing at this time for power; and this is where you fit in. The one party, using the tactics of guerilla warfare, without a central location or a single leader, wants to reinstitute the *reality principle*. These are the Reals and we do not know who they are. Indeed, our presuppositions at present may keep us from ever knowing who they are. That is where you come in. We of the Post-Real Party (PR men and women) must find who the members of the Real Party are and the extent of their activities. The

John sitting in his Funki-Boythorpe wearing a driving mask and striped upper body shield.

Director of AMARCO is one of us, although he is so close to conceptual chaos himself that his efforts are now largely passive. We believe that Laurea is one of the key figures of the Real Party, a guerilla cadre chief of rare and powerful abilities. If she is, she will be reading your field-notes during the day, gathering intelligence on the mask factory operations at the deepest levels, the levels to which we have been taking you. Our aim is to see if we can trace the diffusion of ideas through her to the other members of the Real Party. All our concepts, ideas, methods, theories, and values have been marked with a special dye. As they diffuse, much like the molecules of a single blob of black ink dropped into a large bell jar of clear fluid, we can glean the contour of reactionary responses from opposition members.

Then, he said quietly, we can take the appropriate measures.

I asked him, angered and concerned at the same time, whether or not this was a profoundly dangerous gambit: revealing the most theoretical secrets to the opposition in order to capture the membership.

He responded that it was the only way.

The explanation, and the moral cause behind it, failed to convince me and before he was through talking I was determined to seek revenge, and if not revenge, then institute counter moves that would place me beyond their manipulations and would allow me freedom of inquiry. I thought, as I stood there, half listening to him that I knew what I could do. It might even mean changing masks, mastering the mighty *Enhancer*, perhaps. I was not sure about the details, it was the principle and the overall realization I was after.

There was one, perhaps insurmountable, ethical problem, however. Quite simply, according to Association guidelines, anthropologists must not intervene. The question that burned within me was this:

How could I grow beyond my own professional passivity?

From His Summary of Persons: A Profile of Laurea

Laurea was a tall woman, handsome in her way and an elusive beauty in her youth. I saw her wedding pictures and gathered from them an idea of her physical presence.

Laurea suffered from a rare disease, a sociological malady, diagnosed as *kinesilalia*. Those who suffer from kinesilalia uncontrollably mimic the bodily motions and perhaps the very ideas of the people with whom they interact. Sitting across the table from her at *zoega* in the afternoon, as I would raise my cup to my lips she would raise her cup to her lips. If in a restaurant I ordered salmon in aspic with a rare white wine, she too would order salmon in aspic with a rare white wine. We would eat in a quiet but disconcerting unison. It made me wonder what would happen if she, by chance, should eat alone.

Due to her obvious malady Laurea did not seem like the sort of person who was an opposition leader, a guerilla tactician; there were no maoian political notes in her poetry. Her poems seemed like aerial spires, resembling, in a way, the conceptual symmetry of the whole two-pointed city.

If she was the guerilla leader and the clandestine reader of my field-notes, chronicles, and other documentation, then it would explain why she tampered with the Director's dreams. It would go far toward explaining the chaos he was, maybe inadvertantly, courting.

And there was her kinesilalia. It may have been that she mimicked the information I gathered and her mimicry contained the coded information she passed on to her cadre. They, of course, would transform their intelligence acquired by me through her into the planks of a political platform.

From His Personality Profile Collection

   While gathering data in the local restaurants, I asked men to write short pieces for me describing their thoughts about their children.

First Man

Will the sidewalks hold our children up, over air? They live on flags, colliding in the wind, on the porch stairs. Alive sometimes but barely, breathing in the sleeping hand, they grow up together in knots.
   From someone's dreaming awakened symbols for their faith.
   Easily the world unravels the toy universe.

Second Man

I walked casually into the rubber cell. Wits about me, I fumbled, presuming my bombing heart wouldn't abandon all my bones and landsliding flesh. I bumbled up the walls as if they were floors, felt the picture frame with what had been my hand. I knew the face here was my photograph. My fluid child leaked into the room, past my despair, ignoring the outstretched hands. I tried crying out that she though small would be born again, but my voice lay muffled in a mask of clothes. It could never reach the door. We jelled in one another's arms, desperate to name each other.

Third Man

I ran down the corridor by the water fountain, the woman stuck out her arm. Her fingers are like acid on my genitals. I limp along. Acid chews down my left leg. It grows hollow. My thumping heel. Burning upward and away. The birds in my guts. Small, suave birds ticking in my kidneys, little ravens in my groin. They are careless. Her hand swallows my lung. Her fingers to the elbow breathe for me. We close in the mildewed bed. A child looks up at our second storey from the street and grows up in our presence. We watch him standing there, adult. He raises his hands above his head, arms open as if for the prodigal's return, arms in an arc like the first and wan moon. He looks up at us. We see him begin to cry gently. He murmurs endearments. Feels lacerated by the distance. He knows how far out of reach we really are. He may be singing or sobbing, about to break into languor. We feel for him. Slowly the throat moves up and down behind the disguise. There are other sounds about him in the lilac bushes, under the climbing clematis, resembling flies. He stirs his hands to bring these about. Inside the groomed window I've been swallowed but, thank god, am still alive. She has succumbed beside me molten. We flow along his vision toward him. We lift our new arms, reconstituted, bottled appropriately. We are as entreating as he has been—reborn and masked inside his mute throat, thoughtfully prolonging our agony. We look through his eyes upward again, implore all those shapes, the oddly difficult room we left behind. We wear his lenses now, brimming with tears.

And then I asked children to write about their fathers (one included below).

At night when Daddy lies down in his bed, his brain is connected to a billion tiny conduits that take his nervous energy and channel it all over the world. By his powerful mind he can transport raw materials across the whole space. There is a small connector at the base of his brain which fastens into a plug partially hidden by the bedsheets.

Although I've secretly watched him at night I've never really seen it first hand. An owl materializes once in a while from his different pores. A spirit assembles from all those different openings, so to speak. His spirit is free to roam the earth. I hesitate to say, Like a witch. The owl hunts for its nourishment. With its very powerful ear receptors it can pick up the smallest movements. It pounces on tiny field mice.

Once it had eaten a small mouse. Since my father's spirit can take any shape after it is on its way as an owl, it curiously stopped off at an evening picnic, I think it was, given by some society mavens. A benefit, no doubt. In order to be as innocuous as possible the owl turned into an incandescent light bulb at an appropriate spot on the strung up electric wires. The whole owl burned at least 300 watts. The skeleton of the mouse burned as the filament. Due to the very high intensity of light, only those wearing shaded masks perceived the little mouse's skeleton shining in the owl's stomach. They failed to draw anyone's attention to it.

In the morning over breakfast, Daddy sometimes seems slightly wasted. This morning I noticed as he held a white porcelain cup of *zoega* that from the cuticle of each of his fingers miniature feathers were growing in orderly fashion.

From His Chronicle: City Culture

I am half-way through my field stay and have taken off several weeks for rest and recreation and to summarize what I know of the city and its people. A good summary will allow me to formulate my next moves, try to assess what I do and do not know.

My concise list of their culture is far too provisional, but I have discovered some very important features of city life. The brief review of my experiences here helps me orient myself within the overwhelming welter of people and situations I face.

i.   Masks are central to the life of the people. However, there is no attempt by one person to impersonate another.

ii. In a masked society, deeds are substituted for the facial expression of emotions. Does this not lead to craziness in behavior?

iii. Every entry in the Yellow Pages is a subheading of masks.

iv. The Medical Prosthetic Masking Association (MPMA) is the most powerful cross-cutting group in the city. The surgeons are in direct competition with the mask architects because they want all masks to be made of muscle, facial tissue, bones, nerve nets, and capillaries.

I see no resolution to this conflict.

v.   The Forensic Prosthetic Novelists are those persons who invent unneeded prose based upon fictional autopsies and fictive pathologies. The fictive pathologies only arise when totally gratuitous devices have been installed in or on characters which force them to pursue lives they would otherwise have avoided like the plague.

vi. I must pursue the story of the masked, hence quasi-anonymous, bureaucrat who spends his entire life removing one word successfully from the dictionary *without getting caught*. What, for example, does he do in his spare time? What is the impact on linguistic drift in such activity?

vii. There is no word for "culture" among these people. That is, they have no ethnic diversity. As a result all differences between humans has to be imagined. They have, through the many worlds hypothesis, freely imagined people other than themselves through certain devices invented for just that purpose. The most important of these is the bio-active postcard that portrays imaginary landscapes complete with an autochthonous sense of place.

viii. I must acquire a more thorough knowledge of the psychology of masked populations. I must discover the calculus of pathologies of masked peoples.

ix. Masks can be equipped with burglar alarms, anti-nuclear devices, warning systems, heat sensors, and blood vessels.

x. I believe that part of the secret of the motivational life of the city dwellers is not the Oedipus complex but the continuous search, entirely unconscious, for Ontological revenge. I detect a great deal of repressed anger in people for having to continuously reinvent themselves.

xi. Even the individual teeth are masked among certain professionals.

xii. The sacred center of the cultural system is underground. It is not in the aesthetic (religious?) section. The theoreticians have it. That is not put quite accurately enough. The theoreticians are creating it. The cultural focus continues to elude me. As long as it eludes me I will be unable to get out from between the warring political parties. I must attack the creative process of the scientists, it looks like. Go to the heart of the theory unification project. What is their basic idea?

From a Fieldnote Entry

After talking with a number of theoreticians at several of the underground levels of abstraction and telling them that my field experience would not be complete without it, I convinced them to let me try on one of the *Enhancer* masks. John was on my side in this and used his considerable influence on my behalf.

The only available mask was a prototype of a most recent design and, they warned me, all the bugs were not yet ironed out.

When I get into one I will log the running reaction to it that I have. [Later addition to the fieldnote: I decided in advance that if I put the *Enhancer* on, I would set my strategy into motion—I would actively seek vengeance for being set up between two opposing factions and to hell with the ethics of the Association. They would all get to see an angry anthropologist at play with peoples' basic cultural beliefs.]

107.2 I am completely encompassed over the head, shoulders, and back by the *Enhancer* and, although it has not been activated to normal levels, I feel it begin to penetrate me, probably fusing with the epidermis, maybe deeper.

107.3 The signal was given by a lab assistant and they are activating the mask, but my arm movements are less restricted. I feel the beginnings of the full symphonic thrust of this thing.

107.4 At a pleasing harmonic volume I have the feeling that I am sitting with my instrument right in front of the conductor surrounded by all the other instruments—strings, woodwinds, brass, percussion, voices. . . .

107.5 I have just become the conductor as well as the entire orchestra, but completely from within. The symphonic flow and my stream of consciousness are one. When I abruptly change thought there is a kind of surge, the orchestra veers off, then very quickly gets back onto the direction of my thought, then amplifies it like crazy.

107.15 I am on the way to a high level Research and Design seminar somewhere deep beneath the city. Walking is even euphoric and deeply polyphonic. I am dampening my heartbeat because it is interfering with my ability to think.

107.32 One of the scientists wearing an *Enhancer*, with its semi-gloss skin of royal blue, is using the blackboard to summarize his concepts with a diagram. He is reviewing the evolution of the physical-biological-human conceptual universe to the *N* of now, and beyond. The other theoreticians are nodding, sometimes arguing over a trivial point or shouting encouragement.

108.00 The basic idea is crystal clear and comes in two parts

$$t \longrightarrow -t$$

and

Strange Attractors $t \longrightarrow -t$

where *t* is time and the arrow is moving so we are moving, as a universe of cargo and beauty toward less time. The Strange Attractors are the source of baker transformations (I wish I had a *zoega* and sweet roll right now)—and these transformations, which are regions of chaos-order, run or drive the universe, and the events inside these masks.

The idea is that the evolving universe cannot reverse itself. It accelerates madly toward its own future annihilation.

108.01 My mind is drifting toward a symphonic review of my political situation and these damn theories of the Post-Real universe.

WAIT!

It's hitting me. My *Enhancer* has kicked in at another level and is keyed to my anger. The timpani and the woodwinds are going wild. I realize exactly what I can do.

108.02 All the scientists in the room, thirty-two of them, are listening as I insist on using the black board. They finally say okay go ahead.

109.00 I write, using a fresh piece of chalk,

$$t \longrightarrow -t$$

and there is no reaction. But now I begin to elongate the arrow

and put a *t* at each end:

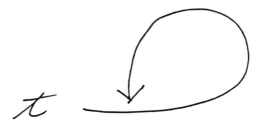

There is some amusement and hostility which my mask and I enjoy—like all the vanilla one can smell. One scientist says,
"See he is making the age of the universe much longer now."

109.01 It is not just the stretch of time I am after. By using the power
augmented by the mask I can treat time as elastic by injecting phenomenal amounts of human subjectivity into it. I do not know if anyone in the room is following my train of thought or not. With this next
move I will have them writhing in their seats due to the novel application of the elastic principle. I decide to loop the arrow of time back
upon itself, bringing the future home to the *N* of now.

The mask and I swell to the ear-stinging crashes of the full orchestra—we are moving as one. I am sweating profusely inside my mask
but it is well drained. Swinging time around takes all the strength I can
muster. I begin to question whether or not I can swing the end of
the arrow back. It is taking brain bending effort. What if I fail at it?

I push the thought from my mind. I am flagellating the *Enhancer* and
myself. There; it is coming around

109.03 Two scientists are screaming in rage and fear: they know what I am doing. Very bright and quick. A third man, anxious and defensive, pointlessly shouts above the clamour,

"That's a hermeneutic circle he's making, look out!"
I just laugh because he is so completely wrong.

Each one in the room now realizes what can happen. With any piece of chalk, on any blackboard or sidewalk, anywhere in the city, even possibly without the *Enhancer*, I can bend the arrow of time around toward the present. Poof. Such a move, demanding as it is, is much more devastating than any threat to them from the Real Party.

The room erupts here and they all speak out with a voice as terrible and impotent as in a nightmare,

"What do you want from us, just name it?"
I have them exactly where I want them and I say in a flat voice that they used me; and if they do not take me out of their imaginary political conflicts, I'll erase the whole conceptual edifice with a single loop.

From a Fieldnote Entry

16 May. The theoretical section voted to make a formal apology for trying to use me against the Real Party. They discussed reparations last night in closed session and today they have asked me, through John, if they might implant a gift in me, as a token of their sincerity. . . .

    I have agreed to the operation, although I despise the prosthetic medical profession. . . .

ACKNOWLEDGMENTS

For their care and close readings I would like to thank Ben Miller, Sam Bass Warner, Jr., Anne Spirn, and five colleagues with whom I met at Auberge des 4 Saisons in the summer of 1987 to discuss each of our writing projects: Billie Jean Isbell, John Stewart, Paul Stoller, Barbara Tedlock, and Dennis Tedlock. Bruce Grindal's stimulating understanding of *The Masks* added to thinking through this book. By providing a steady fund of ideas John Szwed helped immeasurably in my study of Black American street life and more widely, of American culture itself. I would like to mention a special thanks to Patricia Smith for her advocacy and editing.

INDEX

Merion Square Hardware, 66
Miller, Benjamin, dedication, 45, 117
miniature planetary surface, 102
Miz Mamie, 25
Mobil Corporation, 68
modernity, 53
Momma, 23
monopoly, 5
Moon, 23, 26
Moorer, Admiral Thomas, 62n
Mrs. Smith, 10, 11
myth of discovery, 58

Nerlich, Michael 6n
the new, 5−6; and colonization, 6; and
    corporations, 6; giddiness of, 12

on the street, 7; as humorous theater, 7
Ontological revenge, 111

Parsons, 42
Patterns of American Culture, 2
Paul, 25
Penn, William, 2−4, 11, 60; colonial pro-
    prietor, 2; promotional map, 3; promo-
    tional pamphlet, 4
performance on the street, 26−27, 32
personality profile collection, 108−109
Philadelphia, Pennsylvania, 7, 52
Pig, 23−25
poetic and scientific ethnography, 73
poetic inquiry, 12; landscape, 52
poetics of cultural inquiry, 13
Police Commissioner Rizzo, 17
political economy machine, 35
post-real universe, 103, 113
power, 61; corporations and human lib-
    erty, 67
pragmatic social form, 58
President Reagan, 62n
Prigoginian instabilities, 43n
Prince Philip, 46
private enterprise, 4; and poetry, 56
private sector, 2; entrepreneurs of, 7; *see*
    sectors
privately chartered corporations, 2
production processes, 35
profits, 2, 4
proprietorships, 2
public interest, 4

Quaker, 52
Queen Elizabeth, facing p. 1, 6
quiz, 25

rap music, 74
Rappaport, Roy, 34n
reality principle, 104
representative government, 4
rhetoric of science, 59; visual, 4, 66; writ-
    ten, 66
Rivers, W. H. R., 8
Rockefeller Foundation, 62
Rolls-Royce, 31
Rose, Dan, 26n, 35n
Roush, Gerald, 31
Runyon, Marvin T., 60−61

SAAB jets, 77
Schama, Simon, 67
Schechter, Danny, 74
science and corporations, 72
scientific method, 104
scientific prediction and positivist's belief
    in, 104
scramble, 20, 21
sectors of the economy, 35, 37, 61, 62, 71;
    and colonization, 60; as controlling
    mechanisms, 35−36; energy shift, 37;
    for profit, 35; nonprofit, 35; not-for-
    profit, 35, 42, 51, 59; private, 35, 63;
    public, 86
Silver Fox, 74
Sims, Ivery, 23
sites of exchange, facing p. 1
Situation, 23
Smith, Adam, 2, 63
Smith, Hedrick, 62n
Smith, Patricia, 117
Smothers, Ronald, 60n
Smythe, Sir Thomas, 1
social form, 6, 35, 58; capitalist, 33−43
Society of Marchants, facing p. 1
Soderlund, Jean, 4n
South Philadelphia, 16, 30−32, 69, 78
southern Chester County, 46
Spirn, Anne, 117
Stallybrass, Peter, 66n
Steinberg, Leo, 68n
Stevens, Wallace, 2, 52, 54−58, 69, 72;
    his dual landscape, 56